PHEASANT
JUNGLES

PHEASANT JUNGLES

BY
WILLIAM BEEBE

First published in the United Kingdom and in the United
States of America by G.P. Puttnam's Sons, 1927

Published in the United Kingdom in this edition by the
World Pheasant Association, P.O. Box 5, Lower Basildon,
Reading, Berks RG8 9PF, 1994

British Library Cataloguing in Publication Data

A catalogue record for this book is available from the
British Library.

ISBN 0 906864 05 4

Cover illustration: Cabot's Tragopan by R. David Digby

Produced by Alan Sutton Publishing Limited
Printed in Great Britain by Butler & Tanner Ltd.,
Frome, Somerset

PUBLISHER'S NOTE

The great 'naturalist/scientists' have often supplemented formal publication of their results and findings with more popular accounts of their travels and adventures in the field. Directed at a broader audience, such books have always played an important role in winning hearts and minds for the conservation cause. William Beebe's Pheasant Jungles, long out of print and difficult to obtain, is surely a classic example.

Beebe's most prominent achievement during his years as Director of Tropical Research at the New York Zoological Society, was the four-volume *A Monograph of the Pheasants*, published during 1918–22. It remains unsurpassed as the most comprehensive study of those diverse, beautiful and wildly spectacular birds. Through the sponsorship of the society and the munificence of Colonel Anthony Kuser, a member of its board of managers, Beebe was able to undertake a lengthy field research expedition to collect data for the monograph. This trans-Asian odyssey took him to Sri Lanka (then Ceylon), India, Burma, China, Japan, Peninsular Malaysia, Borneo and Java. Beebe pursued pheasants whenever possible, alternating between the comfort and privileges of colonial life and the privations of wilderness exploration, from 26 December 1909 to 26 May 1911.

Pheasant Jungles is a selection of Beebe's pheasant-tracking memoirs and experiences during this seventeen-

PHEASANT JUNGLES

month trip. Capturing the excitement of the solitary
pursuit of these scarce and secretive birds, it also offers
insight into the (sometimes dangerous) experience of
Asian travel at a time when wild places remained largely
untouched by the ravages of development. The characters:
hunters, trackers, porters, cooks and servants he met
along the way receive lively attention and his musings
during long days alone in the field are candidly revealed.

The book has been published under the auspices of the
World Pheasant Association and should be of interest to
each constituency of the modern-day pheasant cult:
aviculturalists, ornithologists, conservationists and
devotees of what has become known as 'world hiding'.
While the text of this reprint is identical in format to the
original, the series of eight magnificent plates kindly
donated by artist Timothy Greenwood and the cover plate
by Ron Digby are a welcome addition. Even in Beebe's
time, pheasant numbers were diminishing. Threats to
their populations have increased enormously since that
time. Today, some species may be numbered among the
rarest birds on earth or are apparently extinct in the wild.
Since its formation in 1975 the World Pheasant
Association has tackled the difficult task of assessing
pheasant conservation and has initiated a wide variety of
projects towards this goal.

In its twenty years of existence, the World Pheasant
Association has grown from a small body of pheasant
enthusiasts to a truly international conservation
organisation which has funded and supported work leading
to the creation of national parks and wildlife protection

PUBLISHER'S NOTE

areas specifically for certain endangered pheasants but beneficial for all wildlife living within the same habitat.

In its early years its policies were greatly influenced by another great contributor to our knowledge of the pheasants, the late Dr Jean Delacour. Delacour's *Pheasants of the World* has become another great classic of gamebird literature and he was the first President of the World Pheasant Association. His successor, Professor Cheng Tso-hsin, the doyen of Chinese ornithology, also has had a great influence on the development of the World Pheasant Association and it is no coincidence that this organisation has a strong and influential Chapter in China where over a half of the worlds pheasants can be found. Through this Chapter the Association is ensuring that none of China's wealth of pheasant species are forgotten or neglected.

Profits from this reprint of William Beebe's original work will all be going to support further research and positive action to ensure that all the world's pheasants survive in their jungles – William Beebe would I am sure, have approved. Anyone who wishes to further support or know more about the work of the World Pheasant Association should write to the World Pheasant Association, P O Box 5, Lower Basildon, Reading, Berks. RG8 9PF.

ROD MARTINS
Norwich
31 August 1994

PREFACE

When I spent seventeen months in the Far East gathering material for a Monograph of the Pheasants I naturally devoted all possible time and energy to the accomplishment of this object. But the human senses are not wholly concerned with direct impressions, and sometimes the oblique, corona-like visual and aural contacts are afterwards all the more vivid for being at the time semi-subconsciously received.

Portions of the chapters in this volume, have appeared in *The Atlantic* and *Harper's Magazine,* but all have been rewritten. The natural history of the pheasants I have recorded elsewhere. These pages have to do with a few of my adventures, servants and thoughts as they came to me in Ceylon, Sikhim, Garhwal, Burma, Tibet, Yunnan, Pahang and Borneo.

This was the first important scientific undertaking which I made as Director of the Department of Tropical Research of the New York Zoological Society.

W. B.

CONTENTS

COLOUR PLATES

All the colour plates are from original paintings by
Timothy Greenwood.

Following page 90

Following page 116

Following page 142

ILLUSTRATIONS

ILLUSTRATIONS

xvi

ILLUSTRATIONS

xvii

ILLUSTRATIONS

ILLUSTRATIONS

He lived for many months in the New York Zoo.

A member of the group of Insectivorous Mammals, able
to scale through the air for many yards on its parachute of skin.

The Dramatic Chief of Sin-Ma-How

Pointing out the best stalking ground for the rare pheasants which live near the meeting place of Burma, Tibet and

China (see page 122)

PHEASANT JUNGLES

Pheasant Jungles

I

THE GATES OF THE EAST

GOING over Niagara Falls in a barrel has now no terrors for me; the memory of two wing-slips and a vicious tail-spin has been made more vivid; the experience of being fired from a torpedo tube is not unimaginable—for in His Majesty's mail boat *Isis,* I have wallowed and plunged through a forty-eight hour Mediterranean cyclone, from Brindisi to Port Said. Only one other experience has ever laid me low—a typhoon and a junk in the China Sea—but then I had at least an unlimited supply of ships' biscuits.

These thoughts came to me in the heart of a hot tropical night when I took a blanket from my stateroom and went up on the deck of the *Lady McCallum* to sleep. The *Lady McCallum,* a small, compact, untidy coast steamer from Colombo, was bound for Hambantotta, Ceylon. She was true to her type over all the world and appeared to take no pride in her work, moving along at a negligible rate amid a generous creaking that arose from some mysterious depths amidships.

Her engine must have been a devastated and haphazard affair, with no remnant of self-respect; while her berths, her superior berths provided for first-class passengers, were intolerably, inhumanly hot, despite the noisy electic fan directly overhead.

Not that there was anything extraordinary about these facts. The only remarkable fact was that, as I walked out upon her narrow, forsaken deck, and saw above me a cluster of low stars appearing and disappearing behind her rolling funnel, I became suddenly aware that at last, at this particular moment, I had come to the real beginning of my trip after pheasants. There was something incomprehensible about this sudden conviction, and also something a little absurd, since I had already covered several thousands of miles of my journey. But these appeared preliminary when I knew that just ahead, somewhere beyond that expanse of black water, was the little harbor of Hambantotta,—the eastern gateway to the jungle beyond. It was undeniably true that some months before I had set out from America, and that this departure marked the lawful beginning of the expedition. However, when viewed from the deck of the *Lady McCallum,* that distant episode appeared somewhat fictitious. Intervening events had more of reality.

My last pre-*Isis* terrestrial memory was of purchasing, in the dark, some Italian picture postcards, half of which proved to be blank, brown paper. This was on the gangway between the

4

transcontinental express compartment and the *Isis,* called by courtesy a steamer, while in reality it was a cross between a half submerged torpedo and a gravitationless turbine.

I have been in all sorts of storms, and in all manner of boats, but never in a combination so irresistible, so potent, so fatal. As we left the harbor of Brindisi—if it has a harbor—we seemed to acquire a sort of planetary impetus which carried us straight on for two eternal nights and a brace of everlasting days: or else the *Isis* must have had self-feeding engines and a self-steering wheel, for whenever, between agonies, I crawled about on intermittent, stumbling forays, I discovered unhappy stewards, ill seamen and disabled officers. At the sight I experienced the unholy joy of unexpected companionship in misery! I smiled a wan heartless smile when I viewed the all but helpless captain; when a stoker staggered to a breathing hole, white even beneath his grime of toil, I was wholly unsympathetic; I openly rejoiced at the collapse and low moans of the ship's cat, and on the second day I watched fascinatedly a family of six cockroaches crawl slowly from behind my cabin's mirror, creep out upon the white doily, turn hopelessly upside down and expire. My entomological instincts suggested that it was the wind-blown bug powder and not mal-de-mer which had wrought this wholesale orthopteran demise, but the circumstantial evidence was strong and at the time comforting to my feelings. The cockroaches, after all the other victims, gave to this new physical horror an almost universal fatalistic aspect, as of rain on just and unjust; so were all we tenants of *Isis* stricken down, both vertebrate and invertebrate.

In a lucid interval along about the fourth day —or so it seemed, for time and space had deserted the world, swallowed up in motion—I had a Noahlike thrill, for through the watery torrents swirling across my port-hole, I seemed to see something other than liquid,—a brown smudge resembling that phase of Earth called land, a substance which, long, long ago, I had actually trod.

I unbuckled my graflex and with infinite pains crawled up to the deck, and took a photograph, whose horizon proved that gravitation had followed in the wake of time and space. Something dragged itself along the rail, a something which in a sane world might have been a steward.

I screamed in his ear: "What land is that?"

He gave me a look of mingled horror and hate, and gasped "Greece!"

We both collapsed and the *Isis,* unattended, kept on her way, a way which at one and the same time utilized all three possible planes, while within us, we knew that a fourth dimension was at work in this horrible world.

I spent long stretches of time gambling with myself as to the arc through which my hanging clothes would sway; sounds too, were absorbing, if somewhat misinforming. I was quite certain that I heard compartment after compartment broken in by the force of the waves, the engines were dismantled again and again, once the anchor was driven completely through the side of *Isis,* while four times we landed full force upon a jagged Grecian rock: At least my ear hinted at such things, but still we forged ahead, vibrating, revolving, leaping, sliding.

I thought of past sins and pleasures, of events and persons. One vision was of my last near shipwreck, of the time I went to Atlantic Highlands to purchase ostriches. Like Macbeth's peripatetic grove, and Dunsany's ambulatory rocks, this errand was unreasonable enough to portend trouble, and trouble came swiftly. Just outside the Narrows, one of the most sudden and violent storms which ever swept New York caught our crazy semi-ferry-boat. What had been some ten respectable women with exactly as many infants, speedily resolved into ten prostrate, helpless beings, while ten jolly little babies rolled and sprawled about the floor of the saloon. I tied many chairs together and dropped the small swarm into the enclosure. It was interesting to discover a quality of agglutination which I never knew was inherent in infants. Whenever in their involuntary revolutions two or three came together they seized upon one another and thereafter rolled and crooned together. They reminded me for all the world of our single-celled ancestors *Volvox* or *Gonium,* rolling across the field of view on a microscope slide. As the

7

floor rose up in its endeavors to become a wall, the entire nursery revolved toward whatever wall at the moment seemed to offer most promise of becoming a floor. Of the babies and myself not one was ill, not one wept, and when finally, the half wrecked old tub was docked, I left the semi-conscious parents endeavoring to collect the hairpins, infants and purses which bore most resemblance to their own, while I went forth into the storm-washed Jersey air in search of my ostriches.

But there were no babies on the *Isis,* to keep up my morale, and my chief concern was to achieve some new and untried position in my berth, and my only regret was that I could not die with honor from the attack of wild beasts while studying pheasants, or at least furnish a meagre stew for cannibals, instead of expiring by slow disintegration upon the high seas.

At one interval of internal calmness—a calm which seemed a prelude to the escape of the ego—my mind went back exactly one month to my departure from New York. How kindly the wintry Atlantic had treated the Lusitania, how regretful I had been to leave her. And my amusing adventure with the Scotch custom officer at Fishguard when striving to make the last train to London. He placed his hand upon the topmost case of my mountain of luggage which happened to be one of my ammunition trunks, and the following conversation ensued, while the engine was puffing, ready to start in two minutes;

8

"Ha'ye anny spirits, liquors, wines, or whiskey?"

"Not a drop."

"Ha'ye anny cigars, cigarettes or tobacco?"

"Not a smoke."

"Ha'ye anny bullets, shells, powder or shot?"

Hopeless collapse on my part, and, half turning to go back to the miserable Fishguard inn, I told the little Scotchman the truth.

"Why man, there's enough powder just under your hand to blow you to Kingdom come!"

He looked at me slyly for a moment, then with a superior grin, "Ye think ye Americans are pretty smart, but ye canna' fule me with yer jokes."

And he waved my luggage and my contraband ammunition on board the van and with a run and a jump on the step of the compartment I was really off on my round the world search for pheasants.

At this moment a sea-sick steward opened the door, stumbled and hurled a cup of coffee across the stateroom, gasped and fled. Things were reaching a veritable Alice in Wonderland stage.

Slowly the brown coffee stains made their way toward what used to be the floor, and for no reason at all my mind went back to a celebration in Wales, where, in company with other scientific delegates, I assisted Their Majesties, the King and Queen, to open the Cardiff Museum. I was surrounded by Bards in pale blue togas, while next me sat the Arch-Druid in white, with heavy copper oak-wreath and wonderful gold breast-plate. In tune with the wind twanging through the *Isis'*

rigging, recurred to mind the marvelous music of
thirty harps that same evening at the castle of
Lord Pontypridd, when the leader sang a toast to
each of us. The old Welsh words of my particular
verse seemed in accord with this present wild
experience on the reputed calm, blue Mediterranean.

Similar, unconnected memories followed one
after another until I suddenly heard my watch
ticking, and realized that time was returning to
earth. My clothing pendulums gradually ran
down, water ceased dashing across the port, and
with the return of life and hope there arose a
desire for food: in the phraseology of a cinema
caption, "Came the dawn of a new and wonderful
day, in which were obliterated all past pains and
sorrows."

The Captain put his head in the door and roared,
"Not feeling fit, eh; better get up and look at
Egypt." And in heaven it shall be written to my
credit that I refrained from asking the Captain
how he had felt the day before! And the ship's
cat rubbed against my legs with a faraway purr as
if to her the whole thing had been only a tempest
in a teapot, or as her feline mind would phrase it,
a mere cyclone in a cream pitcher.

I reverently gathered into an envelope the remains of the six cockroaches, fellows of my misery,
and going on deck I consigned them to the delta of
the Nile.

As I did so I looked ahead at the low-lying misty

"Moi et Cheops"

Close-up of the author on the summit of the great pyramid

The Cresent Beach of Hambantotta, Ceylon

land and there came a vision of the antiquity of men and boats and cockroaches. Perhaps ten thousand years ago predynastic craft had steered out of the delta, and we may be sure that on board there were predynastic roaches, creeping out from mirrors far different from ours, seeking crumbs of strange viands, dodging assaults from objects unknown to us. But the little roaches themselves were identical with my cabin mates; to the last joint of their ever-waving, inquiring antennae they were the same. And passing back through the centuries and millenniums, before mirrors and boats ever were, before man himself was, we find traces of similar little roaches, living and thriving in those ancient days, hardly changed from the tenants of the *Isis*.

To write of Egypt would be to turn this volume from a pheasant trip to an account of a wonder world of sand: to a memory of the time when I evaded the guards and spent an entire night in the heart of Cheops, alone with the bats and the ghosts, peering now and then through the blind eye-shaft, down which Polaris blinked 2000 years ago, and which now waited patiently for the glow of Vega, about 12,000 years hence. My mind clings to the timid little kestrel crouched on her eggs, halfway up to the top of the great pyramid, on the roughest and least travel-haunted side. Here she sat, and stared and stared with her fierce eyes,— the self-same hawklet which the ancient Egyptians mummified with care, and, with the utmost detail, delineated both in flight and at rest. Again I recall the sandstorm in the desert which tried our camels and ourselves, and the nights in the tents, the one when we were raided by a band of roving robbers— all of whom, save one, came and fled so quickly that they might have been a passing dream; and then the quiet moonlight nights when the daintiest of desert kangaroo mice materialized from the very sand grains in my tent and leaped joyously about me.

But like a resolving pattern coming out of pattern and that in turn from another,—so my mind returned from England to Brindisi, to the *Isis,* to Egypt, to—the salty hand rail of the *Lady McCallum* which I was leaving in the dawn of this tropical day.

It might have been that the light breeze brought with it some subtle evidence of land close ahead, some familiar Eastern fragrance which heralded the presence of a native village, with its palm trees rising splendid and still heavy with the moonless night above a row of thatched huts, and its fishing canoes drawn up like a black battalion along the water's edge. For in the early morning a blue mist that lay close to the horizon took form and contour, becoming a white shore behind which distant trees showed in an opaque emerald border against the sky. This had the quality and unreality of a mirage, and the appearance of each successive detail seemed only to bring new elements of fiction into the illusion.

THE GATES OF THE EAST

The *Lady McCallum* stood in slowly toward the coast, and straight before her nose the native boats, made very small by distance, rode on the bright surface of the water like a colored toy fleet,—the illusion persisting. Then a young Cinghalese appeared from some fastness below deck and put his modest baggage well forward by the rail. The spell was broken. There was no longer an opalescent mirage against the skyline, but land ahead.

One by one the miniature boats assumed character, became individual with a purpose in life; and behind them the smooth beach, crescent-shaped, took on the semblance of a port. Some tall figures came out of the thatched houses and moved down slowly toward the surf. There was something leisurely and unhurried about these people, a certain natural poise which was singularly impressive in the midst of such simple surroundings. This might have been due to many things; it might have been something instinctive, or the result of countless subtle influences; but, whatever its source and its significance, it was something shared in common with the young Cinghalese who had come down from Colombo on the *Lady McCallum* and who stood guard over his baggage where it was heaped against the rail, stood guard over his mean assortment of parcels with that same gentle, almost melancholy air of detachment and fine dignity.

The fishermen, too, who in due time came alongside in their canoes, showed this racial kinship. They lent an aristocratic flavor to the humble job of transporting baggage. They were barefooted, and wore no clothing beyond a very large hat and a calico skirt which was gathered up tightly around the waist and fell in straight folds to the knees. But their faces were sensitive and high-bred, at certain angles almost effeminate—a curious effect which was strengthened when, in the stress of manoeuvring a sail or hoisting heavy cargo, they threw off their clumsy hats and showed their black hair done up, woman-fashion, at the back of the head and topped by a tall shell comb. These combs were semicircular in shape, polished, and a very pure bright yellow in color; so that in the sunshine they looked like the half of a gold crown kept upright by magic, as a symbol of some obscure royalty.

But these Cinghalese were a legitimate enough part of their environment. They contributed a perfect foreground for that Eastern picture with its smooth sparkling sea and its outrigger canoes floating their patched sails. And these canoes were not only harmonious in the general scheme, which was their sole purpose when viewed from the deck of the *Lady McCallum,* but they were examples of a very superior craftsmanship. They were nothing more than the hollow trunk of a tree with a mast wherever convenient, and they trailed a short log on one side for balance, but they were water-tight, built for immortality, and possessed not so much as one nail in their whole ingenious structure. They were put together with pitch and withes, and at certain critical points one part would be sewed to its affinity. To man them and to hustle them about from point to point with the aid of a short paddle was a feat demanding both adroitness and agility; but to have sewed one of them together must have been a task brought to fulfillment by nothing short of pure inspiration.

They were not, however, comfortable. At best they were no more than eight inches wide, with slithery bamboo poles for seats. Any baggage of reputable dimensions extended out on either side, minus support, with an endless succession of waves curling up in a greedy, familiar fashion directly underneath. They created also an almost fatalistic impression of insecurity; a box of scientific instruments in company with some photographic plates was continually moving about underfoot, and a small leather handbag rode from one end of the boat to the other at every intimation of a breaker. It was like some sort of endless nautical game in which the luggage strove to outguess the sea. But like any good game it was dangerous, and a gathering of youthful Cinghalese who had come out from land for the dubious pleasure of swimming in again alongside, only emphasized the general uncertainty. They had the air of adolescent ghouls waiting to snatch up every scrap of flotsam and jetsam before it could sink unduly to some haven in the inaccessible depths of the sea.

But the outrigger made a safe landing, being beached by a great wave,—the one particular wave which had been holding back for this moment, ever since the world or I began, to fling me far up, chip-like, on the sand. The young ghouls came up dripping, and I believe were subsequently hired to carry baggage and various scientific items to the dâk bungalow, which faced the harbor from the verdant summit of a little slope. It was my intention to go straight to the bungalow, interview the chowkidar, and set things in order for the day. But I was waylaid. I saw, far out across a stretch of emerald water, the *Lady McCallum* heading for the open sea. I stood and watched her,—watched her moving slowly under the gray cloud of her own smoke. And such is the working of the human mind, I was sorry to see her go. I had been undeniably anxious to leave her, had been the first lowered to the outrigger below; but I did not like to see her being swallowed by distance over that pitiless expanse of water.

And at the same time I was glad, because that unprepossessing little coast steamer was the last link in the long chain which bound Hambantotta to that other distant world from which I had come. And for a time I would have no need of the very highly civilized codes and standards which governed that world; they would be of little value to me in the jungle where life moves upon so much more broad and simple lines. Therefore as the *Lady McCallum* became smaller and smaller against the low clouds that lay close to the surface of the sea, the horizon line of the work I had to do became correspondingly large. And yet at the same time there was that sense of irreparable loss, that mysterious regret.

I went on down the beach toward the dâk, and long before I was aware of it the conventional Caucasian influences were losing their potency. The natives were no longer aliens wearing strange clothing, but familiar, acceptable figures; each one remarkably individual. Some naked chocolate boys were running up and down the sand in the elaborate manoeuvres of a sham battle; this appeared a natural and a more or less amiable proceeding,—which it was. As a matter of fact, it was just as well that the civilized habits of thought I had brought from my own country let go their hold so easily. For I had not only come into one new world which demanded a new viewpoint, but into two. The first and foremost of these was scientific and had to do with pheasants and every other bird and creature near by; the second was made up of the people, and what they were making or were endeavoring to make out of their lives. A third world, even a phantom world built out of memories, would have been a handicap.

Up at the dâk, I found things well under way. The chowkidar, an old man and uncommonly benignant, had opened up his musty rooms and disposed the luggage around the veranda to his fancy. Inside the low front room it was cool and clean, and a gray lizard, a foot long, was stretched out comfortably in the middle of a canvas cot. I dis-

17

covered later that he lived in the roof in company with some others much larger and two harmless serpents, who could stir up a lively commotion overhead whenever the spirit moved them. This was usually at night, because the lizards spent most of the day running up and down the pillars of the porch. They did this in an anxious, hurried fashion, but with no profit in it, as far as I could see.

The big lizard took himself off at a leisurely gait, and I went on through to the back of the bungalow. Halfway across the yard the chowkidar had built a fire, and with three of his friends was squatting on the ground before it. A black cooking-pot rested on the coals and sent up little puffs of steam which, with the blue wood-smoke, formed a light motionless cloud directly over the heads of the four men, exactly like the table-cloud of a tiny volcano. Beyond them a cactus-covered plain was spread out like a big carpet before the distant hills. The men by the fire neither moved nor talked, and the wind had died down somewhere in the spaces of that wide plain; it was all so silent, so peaceful, that for a moment life seemed to be divested of all its ugly qualities. It seemed incredible that the struggle to live could anywhere assume perplexing proportions, that pain or sorrow were allotted a legitimate place in the world. Then, somewhere above my head, two unneighborly young crows began quarreling; their grievance was obscure, but they were singularly vindictive about it. After all, it was only an illusion that the big struggle had been suspended.

And down in the village proper, where I went in search of a servant, the people were having their quarrels, were facing down their own personal problems with just the same spirit which the young crows had shown on the roof of the dâk. The only difference was that the problems were a little more complex, and not so frankly exposed to the light of public opinion. At one end of the narrow street which was, in reality, the entire village of Hambantotta, some Tamil traders were gathered together around their wares, which were spread out on a square of dark calico. I do not know why this array of gold beetles, done in filigree, and these processions of tiny rickshaws, delicately carved, were grouped so harmoniously on their blue background. Nobody was buying, although the Tamils argued loudly among themselves and seemed to be insisting upon the especial merit of each particular offering. At any rate, every Tamil manifested a robust disregard for the claims of his competitors, whatever they were. The crowd looking on was a nondescript collection, entirely absorbed by what was afoot. If the exhibition was a business enterprise, it was also a small fête, a drama. There was unmistakably comedy, tragedy, incident, and situation to be found in the undertaking, and beyond question there was an appreciative audience. The possibility of selling the beetles was, after all, the least of the affair. It may ha· ṣ been that the traders were rehearsing their arguments, arranging them in some hypnotic sequence which would stand them in stead some momentous day; or it may have been that the little rickshaws were only a lodestone, unimportant in themselves, but like afternoon tea, a means of bringing people together that each might set out his individual views for the edification of his neighbor.

As an outsider I was, of course, totally unequal to a real appreciation of this critical transaction.

The same thought brought the realization that when I should have left this scene, when I had placed a quarter earth between myself and Hambantotta, that I should then see clear, understand more appreciatively.

Now I looked at the little gilt rickshaws and could only try to see them through the eyes of the Hambantottese who had never seen a vehicle other than a bullock cart. To them a rickshaw was what an automobile decades ago would have been to Fifth Avenue or Regent Street.

There is something elusive and eternally baffling about human nature at all times, and when it speaks an alien tongue and conducts itself according to alien standards, the two highroads to understanding are closed. There is no way to reach the inner secrets; no way to disclose the inner motives. At best, there are no clews beyond a few illuminating gestures and the chance expressions that show in certain faces in unguarded moments. So in the last analysis I could do no more than hazard a

The Flying Landing of the Outrigger

Hambantotta Fishing Boat and Its Scavenger Crows

Tamils and Chinghalese Appraising Their Catch

guess of the true import of what was taking place around me, a guess supported by various scraps of information and a little theoretical knowledge of conditions. I saw that the Tamils were short, solid, awkward men, wholly unlike the Cinghalese; and I deduced some tentative estimates of their character.

Sometimes these haphazard opinions about daily affairs were verified. It happened that, after all, I had seen a true view of the Tamil personality at the beetle market. For they are a progressive, sturdy, diligent people, traders by instinct. They adapt themselves quickly to a new environment and are quick to seize every chance, no matter how humble or servile, for advancement. Unlike the Cinghalese, they are neither proud nor sensitive. They work on the roads, dig ditches, and even make brief excursions into adjourning territory as laborers or trackers, if they are assured of its profit to them. Their clothes are a savage array of crude colors and their headdress is a turban of bright cloth. A Cinghalese, with his flowing white skirt and white coat, with his oiled black hair surmounted by the tortoise-shell comb, has an aristocratic and distinguished bearing when placed beside them.

Not that the Cinghalese do not adapt themselves quickly to new conditions. They are too gentle by nature to offer any serious resistance to any advance. But they are not grasping like the Tamils; they are acquiescent. They give way quickly to authority and are respectful and courteous. It seems in the nature of a miracle that the Tamils

21

have not completely overcome them, dominated them, and assumed control. Perhaps it was the imagination of the Cinghalese which stood in the way of this; they foresaw that their only strength lay in their holding close together. But whatever the underlying causes, they have given no ground; their superstitions, their religion, their language have all remained uncolored by this strong, opposing influence. And yet the two people live side by side in a perfectly friendly association which has remained unaltered for generations; and each Tamil speaks two or three Cinghalese dialects, while each Cinghalese, without sacrificing his own tongue, understands perfectly the jargon of his neighbor. Which proves, I think, that it is easier to deduce general facts about pheasants than about human nature.

As a matter of fact, although I had set out to find a servant somewhere in that main thoroughfare of Hambantotta, I took no direct action in the matter at all. Instead, I made a few observations on some scavenger birds, since they were present in large numbers and in every degree of efficiency; and I decided that the hundreds and hundreds of crows I had seen along the beach, as well as those crowded together on the yards and ratlines of the outriggers, were protected perhaps by some religious scruple. This provided a secure though uneventful existence for the crows. Their safety was insured beyond question, and each day they might dine magnificently upon such of the catch as the fishermen found useless for market. It was not surprising that they had become an opulent, sleek, greedy lot of individuals, giving to thieving and all manner of impertinences.

As for the servant question, I later turned it over bodily to the English government agent,—a young official who had been sent out by his government to superintend the welfare of the Hambantotta section of Ceylon. It was a difficult job, which he carried through with great understanding, and a certain supreme patience. There was no other white man for miles in that isolated jungle country, and the work itself was not easy. He was unofficially a judge, a lawyer, a court of appeals, as well as all the lesser legal dignitaries upon occasion. I think that England must be very proud of such men.

The manner of our meeting was worthy of Hambantotta—for it could have happened as it did only when a white man plays a lone hand. The agent had been away at the time of my arrival and for some reason had heard nothing of it. When I went to his bungalow in the evening I saw him sitting at table in formal evening dress, looking almost of undergraduate age, alone except for two servitors waiting upon him with equal formality. My appearance cut through all this external effect, or rather emphasized its need, for he looked at me as if I were a ghost and rushed to me as to his dearest friend. With difficulty he controlled himself, but could not let go my hand, for mine was the first white face he had seen for many months, and as he had clung to the habiliments of London Town for the sake of their morale, he now demanded all I had to give in the way of news of the world—more perhaps for the sound of an English tongue than for any immediate desire for knowledge.

I explained my difficulties to him and he took them over straightway. The servant matter was the least of the problems he shouldered, and he dispatched all of them with amazing speed and thoroughness. When I had been in Hambantotta but twenty-four hours I found myself indebted to him for one Cinghalese manservant, one Tamil tracker, three bullock-carts, six oxen, three drivers, a game license, one boar's skull, one junglefowl egg, five peacock feathers, and two dozen bottles of soda pop. He would also have given me his house, I believe, if it would not have seriously disarranged the governmental machinery for him to move out on such very short notice.

As it happened, his house was an exceptionally fine one for the tropics, with its wide, screened veranda and cool rooms. And I found it particularly pleasing because of the geckos who lived there. I saw any number of these little indefatigable gray lizards, and I liked them better than the ones at the dâk, not because they were smaller but because they were more reasonably industrious and more inclined to be friendly. The long clumsy creatures at the bungalow were so big and heavy that they gave an impression of fixed stupidity, and they were not hospitable. Whereas the geckos were intensely interested in all that was happening, and I am sure that nothing but politeness kept them from walking all over the guests of the government as a sign of appreciation. Certainly they walked over everything else within range, except an alcohol lamp which happened to be burning. Their feet are peculiarly fitted for these excursions, having vacuum padded toes which can secure a foothold upon anything, including mirrors and the ceiling. They have also a quaint habit of striking an attitude and remaining absolutely motionless. This may be fear, or it may be a method they employ when stalking their prey—a moth, or even a bread crumb upon occasion. At any rate they secure some novel effects. At the government bungalow there was a large picture placed at the left of the window overlooking the porch. The light upon it was thus indirect, but I saw that it was handsomely framed in dark wood,—a Japanese frame presumably, since at the upper right-hand corner was an excellently done, very decorative lizard. The Japanese handle such motifs with great delicacy. And even in the dim light it was apparent that this was an exceptional example. I could not help but feel offended when it gathered itself together and went scampering headlong down the wall. However, there was one compensating feature to the incident. It happened that the gecko had given me warning of his intentions an instant before his flight, although I had failed to interpret it. I had heard a low, sweet, tinkling sound as if a tiny bell were ringing in some distant part of the house. Certainly I had not associated it with a carved lizard on a picture frame. But afterward I realized its source and its import. It was a singularly beautiful call, a little like a trill; more than anything else it sounded as if a marble had been dropped on a silver platter and were settling slowly to rest.

When I went back to the dâk, early that afternoon, I felt that my first day in the country had been rather well filled up, that I had thoroughly estimated the possibilities of the village. But I found that, on the contrary, the one great event in the daily life of Hambantotta had not yet appeared above the horizon of affairs. I had failed to consider that momentous hour which marks the homecoming of the fleet. I had passed judgment on the play without waiting for the climax; because the arrival of the boats at sunset was the very pivotal point upon which that native community revolved. I do not believe that a more complex people, a more civilized people, can ever realize the significance of such a landing, can ever appreciate the naïve sophistication which makes these men go down and wait on the beach long before the first outrigger has turned her nose toward the land. It seemed to me that every household must have had a representative there,—some privileged one of the family who would return to tell all that was said and done. For there were old men, old Tamil traders with a fringe of white hair showing under their faded turbans, and old Cinghalese sailors who stood about in dignified groups and talked together in a quiet, reminiscent fashion. There can be no doubt that they made unfavorable comment on the methods of the new generation, and did not fail to mention again the threadbare exploits of their own youth. And there were a few young men who had left their work that they might go down on the beach, and, with the unparalleled authority of twenty, pass judgment on all that was taking place. Three girls were standing together in the shadow of the palm trees that bordered the sand, but there were no others along the whole curved length of the shore; so I judged that public opinion held it that women should not be on too intimate terms with the inner machinery of men's affairs. However, there were small boys scattered about in great profusion; they ran in and out wherever a gap appeared in the crowd, and shoved and shrieked, and shouted back impertinent replies over their shoulders when anybody spoke to them.

And when the boats appeared, racing along at full speed against the cloudy sunset, every one of that yelping youthful horde went tumbling into the surf, and some of the tall young men went with them, regardless of the striped skirts and head-dresses which had showed up so valiantly against the white sand. Other young men ran some rollers into place at the edge of the breakers—rollers

27

which had been made by roping logs together in a very fair semblance of a skidway. Then the crowd began to drop back a little, for the boat had already broken into the rough water near shore and seemed to be fairly leaping along over the surface, with their richly dyed tan sails bellying out in silhouette, first against the blue sky, then against the green waves. They shot through the surf at a perilous rate, so that even when they struck the logs they did not stop, but like Captain Shard's bad ship *Desperate Lark,* sailed on for a bit, regardless.

Certainly there were elements of real excitement in this landing, and Hambantotta looked on in appreciative silence until the last boat was beached, and even until the fish were taken out and laid in shining rows on the sand. Then the old Cinghalese sailors went down and sagely handled the catch, appraising its worth and passing judgment upon its imperfections. And the Tamil traders stood by and pointed out the particularly fine specimens in those silver rows,—knew them instantly for their real value,—because there was a lifetime of experience to give authority to such swift decisions. But it was the young traders who bought when the catch was auctioned, and it was the young Cinghalese who were the auctioneers. Which was but one more proof that, for reasons of her own, life seems to have given all her sympathy to youth and not to wisdom.

The auctioning itself took but a little time. It

was the culminating event of events, but it was passed over quickly and quietly. And immediately afterward, the whole crescent-shaped beach was forsaken, save for the crows who had already swooped down from the ratlines to gather like restless shadows at those chosen points where a banquet had been so generously spread for them. But the sand was still marked up with the imprint of hundreds of human feet; in some places it looked as if the water had come up and washed out those shallow troughs where so many people had stood together, and, receding, had left strange, meaningless marks on the face of the sand. It seemed incredible that so many human beings had so short a time before been united there by one impulse, only to return so quickly and so silently to the monotonous movement of their individual lives. But the crows were proof that the shore had not always been merely a harbor for deserted boats; and behind them the setting sun, showing above two bands of violet cloud, touched up with gold a western window in the bungalow of the government agent that overlooked the sea.

The tropical night had descended quickly, and up at my dâk the new manservant had already made a habitable place out of the front room and was awaiting his orders for the night. He was a tall Cinghalese, about thirty-five years old, who said that his name was Boy. He was capable, deferential in manner, and in all the time that he was with me, regardless of the unfamiliar things he confronted daily, I never saw an expression of surprise on his face. He moved slowly about his work, and was equally conscientious about his cooking and the odd scientific jobs that fell to his lot. If he had any emotions, they were somewhere well below the surface. However, he did a great deal toward getting things in line for the work that lay ahead in the jungle; and it was in large part owing to his faithful service that early one morning three bullock-carts pulled up in front of the bungalow and were straightway loaded with all the equipment necessary for the field.

These carts were commodious, wattled affairs, precariously hoisted up on two wheels. They were cool—though covered at the sides and over the top with woven bamboo splits—but they were not comfortable. The roads were bad, winding in and out between deserted paddy fields, and the drivers would undertake any angle which happened to appear before them. It was not that they were eager to reach the P.W.D. resthouse at Welligatta, which was our destination; it was only one more manifestation of the native tendency to acquiesce in the face of difficulties. I traveled over the entire floor of my cart several times. It was like sliding around under an inverted basket, with the possibility each time of sliding right on out through the hole at the back. This was more exciting with a lagoon underneath instead of dry land, particularly when the water bubbled up under the bed and seeped gently through the cracks.

Hambantotta's One Street

My Bullock Cart Fording a Stream in South Ceylon

THE GATES OF THE EAST

It was undoubtedly a precarious, noisy, unsavory journey. The drivers kept up a running conversation from cart to cart, whenever they were not shouting at the bullocks; and the bullocks themselves wore wooden bells. I was told that these were a warning to evil spirits and leopards and such, and, sliding around behind them, I hoped that they were. They were as clear as trumpets, and gave out abiding resonances. Every creature within hearing must have fled inland for its life. Once, on a level stretch of road, I looked out through my bamboo netting and saw nothing but a termite nest, and very high above this, so that they looked like two black motes above the trees, two Brahminy kites sailing smoothly on widespread wings.

When we stopped at noon the drivers put their food on to cook, then rubbed down the bullocks; afterwards, when they had washed the plates, they hung the dish-cloths and the bullock-cloths one over the other on the roofs of the carts. This accounted for many things.

We were some five or six hours late in getting to Welligatta, which is good time for the East. At the resthouse, the door was locked and a surly chowkidar refused to open it. We argued with him, and I had time to look over my new headquarters, finding it to be the typical whitewashed dâk, with red tiled roof. This chowkidar had no inclination whatsoever to be friendly—in which he was true to type. However, when we made elaborate preparations for breaking down his door, he opened it. Which proved him a coward on top of his unpleasant disposition.

This was not an auspicious beginning, but afterwards Boy took him aside and told him a great many things, with gestures. I do not know what they were, but they converted that keeper into a new man in the space of about five minutes. He began hurriedly to get the place in order, and made various pacific advances. Perhaps Boy had assured him that I was a great physician, this being one of his own fixed delusions, since he had never been able to find any other logical reason for the bottles and cases and instruments belonging to the expedition. At any rate, Welligatta shortly appeared at my doorstep and asked for medicine. Some of the cases needed only a little antiseptic soap, or some healing salve; but for others nothing could be done. The little boys were particularly pitiable, because they were especially brave about their treatment, standing perfectly still, shy and heroic in the face of great mysteries and pain.

There was one other native who came in that day—but he did not live in the dirty community at Welligatta. He was of good caste, an engineer. It happened that the resthouse was in his jurisdiction, and he stopped in to see if things were running well. He was a University man, with a fine mind, too subtle and too well trained for the work he was doing. But he could make no further advancement because of the English laws which set a well-defined limit to the power of any native; and he admitted the wisdom of these laws. But he was a tragic example of the good material which any evolution throws aside. There was no legitimate place for his talents, even after they had been brought to their fullest development. He said himself that it would have been better to have let him alone, to have offered him no chance, since at best there was nothing but a blind road open to him. And he had come abruptly to the end of this. He pointed to his man who was lying asleep in the shadow of the porch, and said that in the East such a low-caste servant, without dreams and without ideals, was better off than his master, who could stand on the borderline of a new country and know the full meaning of what it represented, but must remain helpless in the very face of such a realization. It was the inevitable tragic waste which follows close on the heels of any progress. And this was emphasized, in some way, by the fact that he knew such a process was necessary, that in the end it would work out for the good of his people and his country.

The next day, when I got up before sunrise to start out after junglefowl, I kept thinking of all that he had said, and I could not help but compare him with my Tamil tracker, who was waiting, sleepy, incurious, and ignorant, for the day's work that lay ahead. One had made such great strides, and to no apparent purpose; the other had taken no steps at all beside him. Yet they were both moving, each as best he could, toward some obscure goal. I had come again upon more mysteries in human beings and in the philosophies and laws which govern them, and I was glad to put the whole of it aside and start out into the jungle, where I had work of my own to do.

The jungle was like a big park which began almost at my door—a park with little glades and every once in a while a shallow lake surrounded by dark trees. The tops of the trees showed against the pale, luminous sky, although the low branches were lost in deep shadow. The tracker led the way along a narrow animal trail, and I followed, guided chiefly by the thorns which were lined up on either side, like two barbed-wire fences set to keep travelers well within the path.

The sun had not yet come up above the blue haze that lay far to the east, but a host of flamingos flying high overhead caught fire from the first rays on their wide wings. Then the acacia shrub began to show little lines of gold against the mist, and pink, nameless flowers came out like stars in the shadowy glades.

Down by a triangular lake, that was changing from silver to blue, two elephants moved slowly forward through the low underbrush; then turned, and swung into the jungle. At one side of the lake, where the ground rose in a gentle slope, some axis deer watched them till they had gone, and the coarse grass, springing back into place, had covered up the great marks made by their feet.

THE GATES OF THE EAST

I heard the tracker whisper something unintelligible, but it was drowned out by the familiar scream of a peacock, and looking up quickly, I saw the great bird with his undulating train glide down from a distant tree and disappear behind a little ridge some hundred yards away. I had started out after junglefowl, but nature has a contrary habit of offering the unexpected, so I was grateful enough and began crawling along after him. There is something essentially undignified in such a pursuit as this; but work in the field has nothing to do with dignity or with anything except patience, concentration, and eternal vigilance. All that I had to do was to get that peacock within range, and to keep out of sight. In time, I came upon him, although I did not know it. I saw only two bee-eaters balanced on a low branch directly above me. Then, straight ahead, something moved, —it looked like a dry, gray stalk standing upright in the grass. Although there was no wind, it swayed a little to one side and back into position again; and I saw then the contour of the head and slim neck of the peacock, the first wild one I had ever laid eyes upon. The body itself was almost hidden. Then suddenly he leaped into the air, one single spring and a quick movement of his wings lifting him six feet or more in a half circle, with his long train spread out to make a feathery mist which the sunlight fired with emerald and gold. He alighted gently and returned to his place in the tall grass, where he stood as he had stood before, with his neck stretched out and his head down, watching something,—something of great interest which was completely hidden from me. Again he lifted himself in the wide circle and returned. Then something brown moved swiftly across a little opening in the brush and the peacock trailed it, bringing it to bay again. This was in a clear spot, and I got my glasses up and focussed them. First, a gray blurred circle moved quickly into position, then the beautiful breast of the peacock took its place, perfect in every detail of color and structure. And finally, a little brown vibrating point showed against the sand. It seemed at most only a tiny mound of earth, moving inexplicably. At last I saw that it was a Russell's viper,—a viper with a particularly venomous aspect, broad between the eyes, but flat so that it lay close to the ground.

For fully ten minutes the peacock pursued it from point to point, keeping always at a discreet distance, but making the viper strike again and again. It may have been only curiosity, but whatever it was, the bird tired of it at last and stalked over to the edge of the lake, where he found some food that occupied him for a long time. The sun was by this time higher overhead and reburnished his fine plumage to copper and gold. I stood up to see him better and even before I had straightened he had sensed the danger and was running down the side of the slope, beating his wings rapidly for a few seconds before he rose and flew swiftly over the acacias and into the wooded plain beyond. I watched him until the last moment, and as he moved, the bright light made of his train a wonderful colored tapestry.

It was on this same trail, later, that three important things befell. The first was the appearance of a high-backed tortoise. Just before he came out to meet me, I heard somewhere in the bushes a thin, trembling sound, very high and a little querulous in character. Then the singing tortoise came waddling out underfoot, singing as he came. His back was finely marked in broad patterns of gold, and he carried his shell along with a certain proud gravity. He stopped and looked at my feet when they came conveniently within his range of vision, turning his eyes quickly from one to the other. But for reasons of his own he was not afraid; instead he put up his small leathery head, and as if in salute, sent forth again his clear penetrating trill. Then he waddled off again over an avenue of golden flower-balls that had dropped from the acacia trees which met to form a canopy somewhere far above his head. And in the distance I heard him singing.

The second trail episode came about quickly. I was walking along a little ahead of my assistant when I was suddenly pushed far forward by a strong blow between my shoulders. It nearly sent me off my feet. I turned and was on the point of saying fully what I thought about it, when I looked down and saw a Russell's viper lifting itself to strike. I should have stepped on it if I had been alone, and my pheasant work would have come to an abrupt end. It was not a pleasant experience.

Then, the last day at Welligatta, I had the bad luck to get within range of some water-buffalos. I had been told that these semi-domestic cattle were singularly savage, and, for mysterious reasons, would attack any white man without provocation. I had not been fully convinced, however, or else I had given the matter very little thought, because once I had seen a native driving six of the beasts before him, whistling at his job and twiddling a slender whip between his fingers. It had been an amiable enough proceeding. But when I saw those three buffalos lift themselves out of the high grass, saw them rise up heavily with outstretched heads striving for my scent, some entirely new thought about them went flashing through my mind. It happened also that I had been told that when several of these beasts are together they will not attack any man who does not run away from them. With those three, gigantic, black mounds of flesh already getting underway, this appeared an unusually idiotic contention. I did not make any effort to hold it. I put down my camera and went up a tree. And I stayed there for some time, with the three buffalos charging repeatedly underneath, until a native boy came out providently and drove them away. I know that there were elements of absurdity in the whole affair, but absurdity and great danger sometimes go hand in hand. And

Ovservation Tent for Studying Pheasants

Russell's Viper, – The Plaything of the Peacock

Scavengers of India – Griffon Vultures Racing to a Feast

Eight Hundred Vultures Feeding on a Dead Horse

In less than ten minutes it will be a clean-picked skeleton

these beasts are the greatest danger of the jungle country of the East, and this was the least dangerous of seven encounters which I later had with them.

That night, when the packing was done and my notes were finished for the day, I went out under the stars for a while, going over the details of the trip, and I found that incident after incident slipped into its lawful place in the general scheme. It happened that only two hours earlier a native had come in for medicine for his arm, which was marked up above the elbow by elephant bruise. I did what I could for him, and he went away. But although he was only one out of many who had come up to the house for medicine, because he had come last he stood well in the foreground of events. And it was so with the water-buffalos who had run me up a tree. It was only when I thought of the bullock-carts and the noisy wooden bells, of the dâk bungalow at Hambantotta with the yard where the chowkidar built his fire, of the beach and the old fishermen estimating so carefully the catch which had been brought in at sundown, that one thing after another fell into position. I saw that after all it was only a matter of contrast,—that the values were relative.

And I tried to bring some of this philosophy into the question of leaving Welligatta; but this being also a matter of emotion, it needed a little more time before it would fall into its legitimate groove. I knew that in a week I could look back and see that the expedition could not have remained always in Welligatta, but as it was I found it hard to leave. I looked out over the dark trees which grew at the edge of the jungle and saw the lake between the branches like bars of new silver, and thought of all my adventures with junglefowl and spurfowl, wild boars and civet cats. I also thought of the work I had left undone, and of the people close by who were living mysteries daily which I could in no way understand; and I did not want to leave it all unsolved.

Then I heard Boy adjusting my hammock, which hung at the end of the porch. Since it was already well placed, and needed no readjustment, this meant that he was sleepy. So I returned, and all the unanswered questions straightway went out of my mind. I thought that I had no more regrets about leaving the jungle. Then from far away, I heard a thin, trembling sound, a little querulous. I had not known that the tortoise was awake at such an hour, but I was certain that the last thought in my mind was that although I had come to Ceylon for jungefowl and peacocks and had found them, some day I would return. And I hoped that at such a time I would find somewhere a golden-backed tortoise singing to welcome me back to the East.

II

THE words of the Red Lama came to my mind as I leaned over the railing on the roof of the wonder house at Calcutta,

> Who goes to the Hills goes to his Mother.
>
> Oh! the Hills, and the snow upon the Hills.

I looked out over the golden-gray sunset dust which choked India to the northern horizon, and knew that somewhere Kim and his Lama were doing what they were wont to do at sunset time. For if ever incarnations from books to life take place it must be these two,—so much more real than most half-alive humans whose origin is other than in an understanding brain. After a time the clouds to the north grouped and regrouped themselves as snow mountains, and in the dimming light I almost fancied that I could detect cool, upland, glacier air sifting down over the heat of the plains.

As the tikka-gharry clattered to the door the following day, the prehistoric horse parted company with the medieval hack, and only by leaping the dashboard did the driver keep hold upon the reins. String was sent for to mend the traces

41

and my progress toward the high Himalayas was momentarily delayed. For years a favorite trick of mine has been to shut my eyes and absorb more directly aural impressions, whether of jungle or city, and an essay or even a volume of startlingly dramatic content could be called "Foot-Steps." This must be done before the further penetration of O'Sullivan and the tire trade; while elephants and camels do not play fair in this game. But the rhythmical, hob-nailed crunch of German soldiers, the clack-clack of Japanese *getas,* the ker-clank of horses and the soft flick-flick of a trotting dog's claws are much more exciting when the deadening dominance of eye-sight is temporarily dethroned.

And now, while sitting in my horseless tikka-gharry, I heard the unforgettable, sibilant *shuff, shuff, shuff* of bare, callous soles through the dust. White turbaned men passed, bearing on their shoulders a tiny, canvas-bound body, headed for the burning ghat. My expedition was delayed an additional ten seconds by my driver leaving his trace-splicing to dash out and carry one end of the stretcher for several steps, thereby acquiring merit of sorts and perhaps winning reprieve regarding the sin of delay, for which he read less hope in my face. In savage tribes and in densely populated cities death is more prominent in threat or actuality than elsewhere,—witness weapons and funerals.

There is a saying that so strong is the gravitational pull of the Himalayas on the waters of the Bay of Bengal, that one sails uphill from Ceylon to Calcutta, and I felt myself one with this when finally the gharry got under way, and the few twists of the twine sufficed to drag me as far as the Darjeeling te-rain. In April and at tea-time the heat and the enveloping clouds of dust were so overpowering that my mind went off on wild errands of wonder, and I began by thinking that somewhere in those distant invisible Hills were pheasants going to roost whose lives were fated soon to cross with mine. I then sank into a mood of this strange land, and pondered on whether my prospective pheasants had ever been people, or whether I should ever become a pheasant, or whether—but here a beautiful roller flew in the car window, and my mind abruptly metempsychosed from psychic to avian matters.

This gorgeous bird is a sort of dry-land kingfisher and clad in pale blue and rich ultramarine, with a general effect of wine color. It was unhurt and promptly drew blood from my thumb. For this I retaliated by holding it firmly, examining bit by bit all the wonderful lanceolate plumage and finally tweaking out a brilliant tail feather for a souvenir. I then tossed it into the dusk some five miles down the line.

All this time I was rushing through a land of dust. Dust-hued vultures gathered in tumultuous masses over gray mounds—this was their season of plenty. Through the dense, choking clouds could be seen scattered little concentrations in the form of men and buffalos, who with bits of crooked

43

sticks—all dust—were disturbing clods of denser layers which had not yet risen into the air. It all seemed futile and worthy only of a single phrase— dust to dust. I wondered at the calm conviction of these dust men that, in future days, there would come the rains, changing their ploughed dust to mud and their dusty seeds to living green.

After dark I crossed the Ganges, and then, amid pandemonium, settled for the night in the sleeping train. Strange tribes and peoples fought for place in the third class, and now and then barged into my compartment, and when I roared at them, called upon Buddha, Allah, Confucius and strange hill gods to witness their devastation at making such a mistake. Then the soothing rhythm of the rail music eclipsed all else.

At daybreak and Siliguri I changed into a tiny toy train with a screaming whistle which vibrated to one's marrow. More miles of dust from which there slowly arose an enormous crimson ball. Then we dived into a forest and began to ascend, winding in and out, around spurs, doubling back, zigzagging, always climbing. We acquired the habit of crawling beneath bridges and a moment later by a convulsive twist of our steel vertebræ, passing over them. I fully expected to see the trainlet tie itself into knots before we got through.

First came tall jungle terai with hosts of orchids in flower; then, as we got wonderful vistas of the Teesta and the fast-dropping plains, we reached the zones of tree-ferns and rhododendrons. The

Darjeeling and the Snows of the Himalayas

The highest peak in sight is Kinchinjunga

Nepalese Shepherd and His Muzzled Sheep on Sandukphu – the Mountain of
Aconite

heat waves danced over the breathless expanses we had left, while sheer above, waterfalls dashed down through forests,—dark, cool and fragrant.

Darjeeling was wrapped in dense cloud. I had intended next day to write a long description of my first impressions of the Himalayas, but when I came out on the balcony of my little hotel room next morning, and looked across and across, and up and up and up at that scene which, in all the world, has no equal, I did what strong men would sneer at—I went off by myself for an hour and did what a weak mortal does when, for once in his life, there comes a vivid realization of his earth as a lonely planet floating in empty ether. I was thoroughly possessed by that feeling which Herbert Spencer so well phrased as being "an infinitesimal atom floating in illimitable space." And I wrote not a word in my journal.

I suffer from, or rather am blessed with, a life which is composed of an endless succession of violent contrasts. And now, from the grandeur of earth's mightiest mountains, I was brought to the knowledge of a small, mean phase of human life. The Dalai Lama, the head of the numerically greatest religion in the world, had fled from Lhasa to Darjeeling owing to Chinese persecution, and it was a sight vouchsafed to few to see him pass in his partly curtained palanquin surrounded by a guard of splendidly garbed Tibetan generals. We watched the procession with uncovered heads as one would, were he looking at the Pope, or some arch-priest of Allah or any religion, when a missionary—a woman—broke through the ranks, flung aside the curtains and thrust a handful of tracts into the hands of the great Lama of Lamas, when she was gently urged by the horsemen back to the side of the road. One's feelings at such a time were only shame, and a momentary wish that one's skin were yellow and not white. Such self-control on the part of these armed men at what to them must have been the utmost sacrilege and blasphemy was something to remember.

No one is interested in the details of outfitting an expedition, so please put down this book long enough to look up some photographs of the snows from Darjeeling. You will then know why I omit all description, and on your return you find me in the compound of the hotel watching my head coolie. Tandook making the round of the loads of the thirty-two Tibetan carriers. There were besides, Das, a taxidermist from Baluchistan,—a second cousin in many ways of Hurree Babu,—whose recommendations consisted of a list of examinations which he had failed to pass, together with several unacquired degrees. It is a delightful land where an unsuccessful attempt is counted as honor,—a pragmatic vindication of the old adage about lunar aimings.

Off by himself stood one man with no load in front of him—a tall, turbaned gray-beard, whose calm, gentle, commanding mien might, with appropriate costume, have windowed the personality of a holy-man, statesman or some great artist. Yet this was only Rassul Akhat, my sweeper to be, whose mission it was to "go before and make ready all things." None would eat with him for he was without caste, and sometimes I though he was the most to be envied of us all, for being unable to sink lower, for him there was no book of etiquette. His chief function was to hasten ahead at the end of each day's march, to sweep out the dâk bungalow or prepare the camping place, and have ready the requisite fires. Armed with his broom of office he performed his duties with deliberate dignity.

The morning of my departure was a scene of wild confusion.

"Our loads are all too heavy," shouted our coolies in unison.

"Your loads are all too light," screamed Tandook stormily, first in Hindi and then in a medley of hill tongues which would have won him envious notoriety and established him as the bureau of information on the tower of Babel. His white skirts flew out as he rushed about with long strides, lifting one box after another. The women—for to my surprise six of our luggage coolies were sturdy Tibetan women—laughed, and chattered and watched me with undisguised curiosity. The whole jolly horde was like a troupe of insubordinate children.

Except when salaaming to me, Tandook, during the first two days, was a martinet. Toward the coolies, when not violently angry, he was direly suspicious, yet they bubbled over with laughter

and it was with difficulty that I maintained sufficient dignity. For he was a very absurd figure in
his white dress reaching to his knee and tied at the
waist with a red sash. His long black queue he used
as a whip lash when very angry, and over its origin
was balanced the tiniest of hats tilted over his forehead and kept in place by miraculous means. But
while the coolies laughed, they yet respected him,
and Tandook amid the snows of the Hills was as
efficient a super-servant as was Alladin in the hot
countries.

It was a memorable moment when I and my
string of heavily laden Tibetan women and their
no heavier laden husbands, turned our backs on
Darjeeling and headed northward into the mysterious Himalayas. I watched the two and thirty bent
figures, and as the men and buffaloes in the plains
had seemed like mere coagulated dust wraiths, so
these Tibetans with their coarse, harsh garments
and broad, squat figures might well be bits of their
native crags. They seemed "rocks that walked,"
not of jade but hardy granite, weathered and worn,
as if great boulders, carried down from the heart of
the glaciers of Everest and Kinchinjunga, had
melted out from the moraines, rolled tumbling
down the icy slopes, and before they came to a stop
had been endowed with human form and life by
some whimsical god of the mountains.

I decided to make my first stop at the dâk bungalow of Jorepokri, at about seven thousand feet
elevation, almost the same as that of Darjeeling.

THE PHEASANTS OF KINCHINJUNGA

My caravan reached it by winding trails shadowed by oaks and maples, with thick underbrush starred with white orchids and lilies, all in the lush growth of full-blown spring. Here, for days, I explored the dense forest alone, and studied the habits of the black-backed kaleege pheasant, a beautiful steel-blue, white-breasted bird with the hen clad in red-browns and russets.

One day, several miles from camp, I lay prone upon a huge, flat topped boulder on a bed of damp moss, when a laughing thrush flew down and alighted close to my shoulder. Startled by the sudden whirr of wings at my very ear, I turned and sent the bird into a frenzy of fear, voiced by an outburst of screams which alarmed every creature within earshot.

The terrible silence of fear closed down upon the jungle. Myriads of living things breathed quietly, panted or held their breath, while my thrush continued to shriek its terror to heaven as it fled headlong. For several minutes the moss-hung forest gave forth not a whisper of life. Only the slow flapping of great, deaf butterflies showed that anything still lived within the shadows.

From scouting trips on previous days I knew that at this moment there were several pairs of kaleege pheasants in this neighborhood and a nest of these birds within a hundred yards.

The day was a brilliant one in early spring and the air was cool with the tang of the mid-Himalayas, but although it was high noon, scarcely a ray of sunlight penetrated to where I lay upon the floor of the jungle. Even when the alarm of the frightened thrush had passed, the woods lay quiet, with only the distant sibilant tones of the tiny bush-warblers.

From base of trunk to topmost twig, every tree was draped with a thick coat and with pendants of moss,—long, streaming tassels of green and brown, which softened every outline, emphasized every knot. The tiniest two-leaved shoot, just broken from its acorn, bore its burden of fairy filament, which would increase as the plant grew, asking no sacrifice of sap or light, but only a support upon which the moss could ripen its lowly spores and whence it could, with wider vantage, shed them abroad.

My great boulder jutted out from the jungle floor, lichen-painted and moss-softened and forever shadowed by the dense foliage overhead. Before me seven great oaks encircled a little sombre glade, all leaning slightly toward one another as if met in intimate, solemn conclave. A checkering of twilight sifted through their green, swaying curtains, and now and then a shining drop of moisture fell from some moss stalactite, glistened for a moment as it passed through a ray of light, and silently vanished as it struck the sponge-like carpet of the glade. Just beneath me this carpet was variegated with tufts of graceful ferns, while tangled among the moss filaments of the boulder were masses of acorn conglomerates—a dozen great caps grown

together, some still filled with fruit, others empty
—gone to fulfill their destiny, whether to bring into
being an oak to replace these giants, or to be
crunched by a passing bear or swallowed by pheasant or jay. In the interstices of the boulder's steep
sides, clinging to scanty bits of black mould, stood
little jacks, much like the jacks-in-the-pulpit of
our American woodlands, but gay with stripes of
maroon and pink.

As I lay among such surroundings, hoping for
a view of some of the jungle inmates, the dim light
occasionally grew more dim—still more diffuse.
Then there reached my ears the indistinct murmur
of wind through moss, and following a sudden
shower of drops from the saturated foliage, there
came through the glade, billow after billow of
cloud, faintly veiling the jungle vista with blue.
It had come down the valley from the snows high
overhead. From the glaciers it brought a cold,
humid chill, but on its way thither it swept through
the higher forests of magnolias, and from the great
swaying blossoms on the mountain sides a mile or
more above me, many miles distant, it gleaned a
burden of perfume, and now the air of the glade
was filled with the sweetness.

As quickly as it came, the chill wind passed, the
clouds sifted onward through the waving moss and
the sun shone out, bringing a new wave of warmth
from the valley below which penetrated even to my
damp couch.

A long, low mound in the furry carpet marked

a tree, fallen years ago, and now rotten and giving of its substance to nourish its children sprouting on all sides. Suddenly above this appeared the small, trim, scarlet cheeked head of a hen pheasant. She reached up, snatched an insect from a twig, scanned the glade for a moment and disappeared. The ferns closed over her, but soon, a few feet farther along the log, a fern trembled for a moment as she brushed against it. In a few minutes I knew she must be safely ensconced on the seven eggs which I had already located close to the distant end of the fallen tree. There for the remainder of the afternoon she sat closely—patiently warming the chicks into life—her mottled plumage one with the browns of moss and sodden leaf.

A dainty, green-backed titmouse flew to a twig on a level with my eye and, filled with the joy of spring, burst into song. He raised his crest, threw back his head and shouted *cheep-a! cheep-a! cheep-a! cheep-a!* again and again. No answer came, but he did not lose heart. He had another song in his humble repertoire, and suddenly he changed to a high, metallic *heep-heep! heep-heep! heep-heep!* trembling with emotion the while. Surely if any lady titmouse was within hearing, she could not fail to be moved by this magnum opus. Far up among the foliage many small birds were twittering and some distant note seemed to carry a meaning to him, for after a moment of listening he was off like a shot.

Then two more Himalayan lives touched mine

for a moment of time, to diverge forever almost at once—and two as different as I could imagine. A yellow-backed sunbird appeared before me, as suddenly as if from the clear air, as beautiful as if from some unknown fairyland. Perched in a glow of sunlight almost within arm's reach, the feathered atom was ablaze with metallic color. From its beak to its toe one's eye registered successively green, maroon, olive, bright yellow, green and black, while its breast was of brightest lemon stained with crimson. A shuffling among the ferns drew my eyes away and slowly there lumbered past, seen dimly beyond one side of the glade, a half-grown bear. The black beast made no commotion, pushing quietly through the underbrush and soon passing from view. When I looked back the sunbird, too, had vanished.

The rest of the afternoon passed quietly, although I once had a thrill when two deer came close to me and crossed the glade, with many stops for a nibble at fern-top or moss. One was rufous, one was brown, a sambur doe and nearly grown fawn. Their eyes were lustrous even in this dim light, and together with ears and nostrils never for an instant ceased their vigilant watch for danger. I was hidden and above reach of scent, but not a rustle of squirrel or bird but was noticed, not a movement of shadow or quiver of mossy bough but was tested with sight and scent and hearing. Their life seemed one great fear—one neverending watch for death. And here was I, the type of the most terrible of all their enemies, my gun ready, but with my mind far more murderously inclined towards any of my fellow men who at such a time would have shot them, than toward the wonderful creatures themselves.

The most conspicuous and jolliest of the lesser tenants of this kaleege jungle were golden-winged laughing thrushes, sturdy birds, clad in gray-striped browns, set off with patches of black, white and greenish gold. Vocally, they were usually quiet, but forever making a great racket among the leaves and debris of the jungle floor. They worked in pairs, and from the sound of their progress might have been a whole flock or herd of creatures. Now and then they would leap to a low twig and burst into a rollicking duet—a sudden, startling, mutual guffaw of loud, harsh notes. It seemed as out of place amid the quiet of these dim aisles as the antics of a clown in a cathedral.

The setting sun found many loop-holes in the canopy of moss, and the glade became brighter than at midday, the long golden shafts reaching far in through the jungle, turning the moss to golden lacery and the ferns to yellow-green filigree. New bird voices came to my ears—two, sad half-tones reiterated until they seemed to embody all the sorrow and tragedy of the wilderness. The first call of the coming night silenced the voicing of the day's sadness; the deep gruff *hoo! hoo!* of an owl presaging the still more terrible intimacy of life and death when the sunshine had gone.

One of My Tibetan Women Carriers

Her four husbands carried no heavier loads

Tandook – Tibetan Super-Coolie

From Rhododendron Blossoms to the Eternal Snows

A trail on the Singaleela Range, Sikhim

THE PHEASANTS OF KINCHINJUNGA

Some time later a whirr of wings drew my attention, and there, in full view, a pair of black-backed kaleege balanced on a low, swaying branch. For a brief space they conversed in undertones, each murmuring in the manner so characteristic of all this group of pheasants. The brown hen almost immediately scaled down to the mossy log, took, as before, a single comprehensive look about, and dropped down in the selfsame place among the ferns, going on to her eggs.

The cock bird ascended the maple sapling, branch after branch, and then crossed to an oak and continued to climb his arboreal ladder until he had almost reached the level of my eye. Walking out on a good-sized branch on the opposite side of the trunk he stood for some minutes, looking down, behind, upward, in every direction, murmuring all the while; his vespers an invocation against the dangers of the night. He then plucked idly at a strand of swaying moss near him, rearranged a wing feather and settled down for the night, with a last, low chuckle—one among a hundred shapeless bunches of moss. I dimly sighted his scarlet face along the sights of my gun barrel, but would pull trigger neither for science nor dinner. When the light had grown so dim that he merged with the moss fantasies about him, I wriggled backward, slipped down the moss-deadened surface of the great rock, painfully stretched my stiffened limbs and began my silent dog-trot along the mossy trail toward camp.

PHEASANT JUNGLES

Two days after I had watched the nesting pair of pheasants I passed close to the log where the hen should have been sitting. A glint of white drew my attention, and parting the ferns I found the seven eggs clawed out, and fragments of shell and yolk all about, covered now with a host of angry ants. The havoc had been wrought the night before, and a little careful search showed that Baloo was the villain—either the same bear which had passed me two days before or another of the same size. The footprints and sign were unmistakable. In this case, at least, there was no malice aforethought; he had doubtless been searching for grubs, tubers and berries, and had ambled aimlessly up to the fallen tree. But the sudden apparition of his great paw, which he had rested on the soft moss, had sent the mother pheasant in swift, terrified flight. At the sudden roar of wings we can imagine how eagerly he sniffed the eggs and clawed them out into a broken pile, licking the shells and his dripping paws with satisfaction. Thus had seven little pheasant lives come to nought. For several mornings, I heard an intermittent drumming from this same patch of forest. It was undoubtedly the first hint of the founding of a new home.

On the last day which I spent in this glade of the kaleege, I had another most vivid example of the dangers to which these wild creatures are subject. I reached my favorite boulder at noon and lay for several hours watching the life of the jungle. At first it was unusually warm and quite breathless

—the forest fairly steamed in the unwonted heat. Then a cool breeze sprang up, followed by a sudden bank of dark clouds well above the valley. From these a terrific burst of hail descended without warning. The foliage and moss were torn to shreds as by shot. The pain of the impact was so great that I was compelled to crouch close between an out-jutting bit of rock and a sloping tree-trunk. Holding my hand out for a moment, it was stung and pained as if lashed by a whip. In a very short time the pellets of ice were piled up three to five inches, and untold numbers of forest creatures must have perished miserably. The ferns about the old nest of the kaleege were lashed flat. Two nests, the one of a warbler and the other a flycatcher's which I had been watching, were literally beaten from their supports and their contents crushed. Every blossom was in shreds, not a leaf remained whole, and the forest, from the peace and warmth and life of the full flush of spring, took on the death-like aspect of winter.

While the storm lasted the cold was intense and the downpour was intermittent; first hail in sheets for several minutes, then blue sky and a momentary gleam of the sun through a rent in the swirling gray clouds; next a fierce downpour of rain, changing almost at once again to cruel ice. Such storms kill dogs, fowls, geese, cattle and even men, and the destruction of pheasants and their eggs and young must be enormous.

Winding upward, one, two thousand feet I left

behind the appropriately named hamlet of Ghoom and my temporary home Jorepokri, together with the mossy jungles of oak and magnolias, and entered a forest of blossoms,—rhododendron trees of rose, cerise, crimson and white, with undergrowth of fragrant pink laurel, while beneath all, the soft, leathered soles of my carriers crushed untold numbers of golden-hearted white-petaled strawberry blossoms. Every native arrived at the next camping place with a blossom behind his or her ear, plucked during the heart-breaking climbs without shifting their eighty to one hundred pound loads.

Now and then stray bits of hill humans drifted along my trail, a yellow robed priest from some isolated lamasery, or a Nepalese shepherd with a few sheep, all securely muzzled against the fatal chance of a nibble at a cluster of aconite leaves.

Up and up we climbed to Tonglu, beyond the source of the Little Rungit, a mile higher in air and two months earlier in season. After a night's rest we slipped fifteen hundred feet down into full spring again and then up to the real backbone of the Singaleela Range which stretches on and on to the very heart of Kinchinjunga itself. The two ramshackle huts of Kalapokri were over the Nepal border, and here I found the very home of all rhododendrons—forty and sixty foot trees at their height of bloom. While my pony feasted on its tiffin of leaves, I wandered about glorying in the color, one side of the valley almost solid scarlet and the other thickly flecked with the richest, warmest pink. When, however, I came to examine individual plants, either through glasses or actually by picking the great blooms, I detected at least a dozen colors, among them being white, creamy, yellow, bluish, maroon, purple, rose-red, crimson, pink and scarlet,—all different species. Sixty-two years ago when Sir Joseph Hooker was encamped on this very spot, he collected over two dozen species of rhododendrons.

The trail to Sandukphu wound along sheer mountain sides, and the horses walked on the extreme outer edge of the precipices, so that by leaning from the saddle I could look straight down thousands of feet.

After dinner in the tiny dâk snuggled against the very summit of Sandukphu—the mountain of aconite—I crawled into my sleeping bag in front of the great fire of rhododendron logs. For a while the air was content to murmur and sigh about the eaves. Then there came a louder whistling and by midnight all the winds of the Hills were loosened. Never will I forget the howling and screaming of those Tibetan demons,—moans close about the window and unearthly crescendos swirling past.

When I awoke next morning all was dazzling white, from the snow-capped peaks to the doorsteps of my dâk. Five inches of a May snow storm covered all the primroses and anemones, and Christmased all the pines and spruces. The air just about the bungalow was crisp, cold and quite calm, although the tops of the spruces beyond the summit were whipping. I walked a few steps toward the chasm in front where the utmost depths were choked with cloud foam. My eyes went up to the sky—clear-cut sapphire through the icy air, and one more great thrill of my life came and passed: Everest stood out unbelievably high overhead, a crystal of palest pink resting lightly near the snow chair of Peak Number Thirteen. To the east were all the others, as familiar now as the faces of dear friends,—Kabru, Jannu, Siniolchum and glorious Kinchinjunga itself.

The one overpowering impression was of eternal stability. Here was the highest and here the second highest points of the earth's surface, and here apparently they had been since the beginning of time. Yet, in a limestone cliff, on the very shoulder of Kinchinjunga, over three and a half miles above the sea, are plainly visible corals and shells and the stems of those vegetating starfish, crinoids, marking a time when, for unknown ages, the waves of an unnamed sea washed over all this region.

A great pile of nondescript blankets and rags at one end of the open veranda showed that my coolies were still sleeping. The snow had drifted deep over them but when the big heap of humanity finally tumbled apart, each man and woman shook off the crystals with the same good humor with which they trudged, up hill and down, all day beneath their loads. Their dressing consisted in shaking off the snow; their ablutions were achieved with a few mouthfuls of the same substance, and

their food was a handful or two of rice and dried
meat. They lived the simple life.

The sudden coming of the snow to meet us, here,
over two miles in mid-air, went to our heads, and the
Tibetans sang, rolled through the drifts and threw
snowballs, while we madly photographed and
painted and scrawled descriptions of the changing
colors. I walked to the very edge of the gorge and
peered over. My cap shot up thirty feet into the
air, curved outward and slowly drifted down. I
found out what was whipping the spruces—a
strong, steady updraft which rose, valley-siphoned,
like a wall, leaving the summit quiet. The next
morning it still blew unchangingly, and, little
by little, I leaned far out upon it, much too far
ever to get back if the blast ceased. But it did
not. I leaned upon the wind as I might stretch
out upon a rock. No more astounding sensation
has ever come to me.

I chose Sandukphu as a halting place from which
to make excursions west into Nepal, north to Phal-
lut and on to the gorge of the Changthap, where
Dhanga La rises to a cold and barren fifteen thousand feet, and the eternal snows of the outer spurs
of Kinchinjunga are only ten miles away. In this
region I found and studied the blood pheasants,
the impeyans and the tragopans; here silver-gray
foxes barked in the moonlight and huge eagles
swung past in the chill of high noon; here I had the
glorious fun, the many joys and the few adventures which are always my portion when my whole

mind is on the wary game I am stalking. I often think that if I trusted less to unconscious preservative instincts I would many times falter and fail. After a hard stalk, when I have achieved my object and am trudging wearily but happily campward, I have sometimes become appalled by the going, over which I had previously passed without giving it a thought; in fact I have often made wide detours, seeking for better and safer foot and finger holds.

On the other hand, what promises to be a real adventure often fizzles out in the end, and leaves me with only an anticlimatic tale to tell. Such befell one day in these high Himalayas when I had been caterpillaring along a bitter ridge, hoping for a photograph of a covey of blood pheasants. I had my camera, gun, two Tibetans and some chocolate. Like a young hound I had been tempted aside to follow the track of a snow leopard, and was rewarded by finding where it had killed a cat-bear, the abundance of fur making the identification quite certain. This side of the ridge was knee deep in snow. The top was a knife edge, and crawling over I suddenly realized that the opposite slope had acquired a solid, glairy, ice surface. I began slowly to slip down, revolving as I went. At this time I had in my hands my graflex camera, the corner of which I endeavored unsuccessfully to jam through the crust. At my second revolution I saw the frightened faces of my men appear over the ridge.

As to my thoughts, I can recall only that I was fascinated by the pink and lilac clouds hanging

My Dâk Bungalow on the Summit of Sandukphu

Mount Everest just visible through the clouds

My Drink of Warm Milk from a Hybrid Yak

over the distant snow-peaks. I was evidently too frightened to think coherently. I revolved faster and faster, and then more slowly as I struck a less steep grade, where I spread-eagled in the hope of acting as a brake to my descent toward the edge of the icefield, which I knew gave abruptly to a fifteen hundred foot drop. As a last resort I turned over on my face, when my toe caught in an irregularity, and slipped out; but the other foot went in and held. With my toe grip as a focus I made half a revolution from my impetus, and then hung, head down-hill, almost at the very edge of the precipice. Locking both feet in the depression I lay for several minutes until I regained a little control of my trembling muscles, and then reached around and got my fingers into what I found was the deep, frozen track of my same snow leopard. Two of these foot prints close together gave me sufficient hold for safety, and I broke off the edges and cached my camera. The great cat had evidently walked close to the edge the day before in soft snow, and a freezing rain had, fortunately for me, hardened its tracks to icy molds.

My Tibetans now started to my rescue and one of them chopped out foot-holds for himself half down the slope, and from there uncoiled a rope and began to flick it toward me. I had an uncontrollable desire to look over the rim and see where I would have gone, and here is where I made my mistake, and received a second shock, this time of mortification, for there, not more than eight or ten feet below, was a broad, outjutting, snow-covered ledge of rock, on which I should have landed gently, and from which my shouts would soon have brought help from my coolies. The sheer drop began from that rock.

Still I had a small recompense, for my last action started up the covey of blood pheasants of which I was in search, which skimmed along the edge of the slope. My fingers were too cut and frozen to open my camera so I got no photograph. As I was being hauled up by the men I noticed that the clouds over the snow peaks had lost all the lilac and were only pink. My absurd lot is to have irrelevant facts like these, as predominant memories of such swift passing events as my Himalayan spread-eagle spin.

III

THE HILLS OF HILLS

THE Hillman and I squatted on our heels and gazed at Halley's comet. I knew he was looking at it, for I could see nothing of him—his tousled mat of hair and his rags merging with the grass about us. In a minute he turned his face toward me and it shone dully in the sickly green light. I could see him without taking my eyes from the comet. Then, like the Cheshire cat, he softly melted from view again; and now when I looked directly toward him he still remained invisible. We sat motionless for some time. I did not know his thoughts, and I could not put mine into words. When, at midnight, one looks across five ranges of Himalayas, lighted by the silver of starlight and the dull green of a great comet, thoughts become emotion, inarticulate and without simile. One registers even the absurd details which are often the most vivid mental aftermath of a profound emotional crisis; my little red notebook from the basement stationery store in Vesey Street was standing on edge in the stunted elephant grass.

When I turned to my wild Hillman, I wondered

again what occupied his thoughts, and at last I was
sure I knew. At such times one thinks of the
greatest things in life, and this to him was the
vision of eight rupees, a great sum which I had
promised in return for a pheasant's nest. And I
had lent truth to this incredible thing by actually
showing the eight shining coins. He had communed
for a few moments with my khansamah, who doubtless had confirmed the suspicion of my madness,
and who vouched for no return of sanity, and hence
withdrawal of the offer, on my part.

Somewhere in the purple-black valleys behind
us was sleeping a small herd of sheep and goats
which he had helped to guide over the hills. Each
sheep and each goat bore a burden of forty pounds
of salt, which, as they were being driven down to
the plains to market, seemed an unfair thing to
ask of them. My khansamah spread the news of
my madness, and with stolid faces, unanswering,
the shepherds passed on. At nightfall one of the
hillmen stole back, and with fear in his face slipped
up to my servant. He had dared to violate all the
traditions of his folk. For who had ever exceeded
the great adventure of the annual trip to the edge
of the Hills?—a day or two of timid bargaining,
and, after the Hillman had been shamefully
cheated, a hurried return to the nomad village.
Where this was we never could learn. Only that
it was far to the north, close to the snow peaks
which forever kept apart the Tibetans and the wild
Hillfolk of hinter Kashmir. He was Hadzia.

That was all. And now I knew that, if he was really looking at the comet, the wonderful light it shed glowed to his eyes like the shimmer of eight rupees. And I would have given a second eight and twice eight more to have been able to talk to him in his own tongue and to learn of the hopes which the realization of the eight was to bring to him.

But this was well past midnight and much was to happen before the earning of the eight. For a short space we squatted silent as Buddhas, with no sound of wind in the deodars which dropped down away from us on every side. Then from a side valley came a swirl of sound, a confused rustling, with sleepy chattering and mumbling, and we knew a family of bandarlog was restless in the strange light.

The low, broken plaints were absurdly like the senile mumblings of old, old men. Aged, toothless ones they seemed, whose sleep was the most prized possession left among the dregs of life. And this struck the chord which vibrated through these western hills: age, infinite age. Again and again this thought recurred in a hundred forms, and every incident, every vista had this as a background.

I seemed to rest upon the very summit of the world, while beneath me, file upon file, the ghostly minarets of tree-tops sloped steeply into the translucent darkness. The stars were brilliant, and the luminous cloud of the Milky Way softened the shadows. In the East the great train of the comet was drawn across the sky like a second milky way. At the apex the head glowed with a pale green glare. It was the comet, rather than the stars, which etched into the blackness of night. I watched it with a concentrated fascination almost hypnotic. Here was I in the twentieth century, gazing on this splendor of the heavens—a solitary scientist in the heart of this great wilderness of tumbled mountains. There came vividly to mind the changes which had taken place in the affairs of men since last its train brushed the earth. The continent of Asia was then all but unknown, Japan was a hermit nation of Mongolian islanders, Italy was not then a kingdom, the flag of Mexico flew over Texas and California, not a mile of railroad had been built in Europe, the telegraph and the Origin of Species were unheard of. Then I thought of the importance of eight rupees, and the affairs of the outer world sank into insignificance. My momentary dream passed, for an insistent call, a mysterious, metallic double note, came from the deodars; a sound which was always to elude me, but which, during this and following nights, from dusk until dawn, was to become a constant background of soft insistent rhythm.

I rose abruptly, motioned to the Hillman to follow, and padded softly down into the forest of deodars and silver firs. The mighty columns rose straight from their deep beds of fallen needles. Almost as tangible as their ghostly trunks was the heavy, exciting incense which filled the glade. The overhead foliage was scanty where I chose my next seat, and the light of the comet and the stars sifted softly through the needles, and reached me, diluted but still greenish. My ways must have been wholly mysterious to my new follower, but he had the philosophy of the hills, and without question squatted silently behind me.

Minute after minute of silence passed and then the great conifers gave forth two sounds. Somewhere a sheep bleated, a sudden, abruptly quenched falsetto. My man rose to his feet with a single motion and answered with a low, guttural exclamation. His calm was broken; the shepherd in him dominated. For we both knew what it was. A strayed animal had been struck down by a leopard or tiger. And I wondered, wholly irrationally, whether the bag of salt was still strapped to the victim. Again the Hillman showed his caste, and against the protest of all his trained instincts remembered the madness of the Sahib and squatted again on the yielding needles.

Then it was my turn. From high overhead in the tracery of foliage came a low chuckle. Probably no sound in the world could have affected me so much. It meant that somewhere near by was a roosting pheasant. And it was to find this that I had come half round the world. It was to become intimate with these birds that I had traversed the fiery Plains and had penetrated deep into the heart of this wilderness—these Hills of Hills. So it was that on this first night I was so wholly absorbed in a desire to penetrate some of their secrets that the sudden indication of their presence, invisible but close at hand, shook me like strong emotion. I sat breathless, tense in every muscle.

No further sound came from either the sheep or its assailant; the bird's chuckle was not repeated. But at once other actors came on this wilderness stage. Some creature suddenly rushed up the nearest trunk, and we both jumped. Neither tigers nor pheasants have the habit of scrambling up tree-trunks, but our reactions were instantaneous and illuminating. Hadzia shrank close to me; I leaned far forward, using all my senses and cursing their inadequacy. With this sound the peace of the night ended and the comet looked down upon swiftly passing incidents.

The creature ascended by starts, each movement sending down upon us a shower of bits of bark. Then another animal climbed after it, steadily and more slowly. Silhouettes against the sky showed the long tails of each. I watched silently. The second creature gained on the first, and suddenly a dark form hurtled through the air toward me. It swooped between my head and the nearest tree, a claw brushing my cap as it went past. It crashed into a low shrub and clambered nimbly to the top. The second animal ran down the trunk a short distance and also leaped or fell with even a harder crash on the other side of where I sat. It ran to my very feet, when I flashed the electric light full upon it, and with a snarl it drew back, showing the sinuous body and cruel teeth of a pine marten. It slunk off into the blackness behind, but not before other actors had made their presence known.

A third animal ran along a branch overhead and awakened pandemonium in the shape of a pair of koklass pheasants which blundered off through the trees, squawking at the top of their lungs. Reaching the end of the branch, the giant flying squirrel, for such it was, sprang into the air. In the dim comet light its wide-spread parachute looked as large as a blanket, and I involuntarily dodged as, with a resounding thump, it struck the tree nearest flying squirrel number one. Then it called—a sudden, sharp, loud squall, ending with a clear metallic note, repeated again and again. The other squirrel answered with an infantile whine, and I read the whole story—the near-tragedy which had been enacted in the gloom of the forest; the murderous pursuit of the marten, the awkward attempt of the young flying squirrel to sail to another tree, the daring but unsuccessful leap of the marten. Then the mother coming, not to the rescue, for these gentle creatures have no weapons of offense, but at least, relying on her activity, to scream her fury at the terrible pursuer. Her flight had been made between two trees at least a hundred feet apart. I had seen her skilful twist and break as, passing against the stars, she steered unerringly for the trunk ahead.

Such was my first meeting with the koklass pheasant, although at the time, in the exciting onrush of other creatures, the flight of the birds was momentarily forgotten.

The pleading cry of the baby squirrel still rang in my ears. It voiced pitiful helplessness, utter inexperience. And this tiny creature's fear and babyhood were all the more pronounced amid these great living trees which had stood here so quietly for centuries, typical of the extreme age of life; and beneath the great glowing comet which stood for the rhythm of recurring cycles, the only semblance of life which the inorganic world can boast. And now the baby squirrel rested in safety close to the great mountain slope which mirrored the earth age, that span in eternity which has neither life nor rhythm.

I turned to my Hillman and found him watching me calmly, incuriously, waiting for the next move of the Sahib. I had been glad of his company, but I wanted him to be ready for pheasant nesting on the morrow. So I placed my head in my hand, simulating sleep, and motioned him toward camp; and without word or sound he rose and softly climbed the slope.

Deep into the pungent forest I crept on noiseless moccasins, down, down, until the eerie shadows all lay slantwise, and there with my back against a spruce I waited for the dawn. The air suddenly filled with little ghostly forms which, while they hummed close to my face, were invisible in the dimming comet light. Finally my eyes forgot their civilized limitations. Desire and intensive effort slipped the scales away, and I began to detect the pale gray form of countless moth-millers flitting about. This discovery was absorbing, for I had learned that these millers formed, at this season, the principal food of the wild pheasants, there being twenty or thirty at times in the crop of a single bird. And now the little flyers interested me for themselves. In daylight I had known them as dull clingers to bark and foliage, when disturbed scuttling beneath a leaf. Now they were swift and skilful of wing, taking an active share in the night life of the Hills. Their wings hummed so loudly that I thought I was resting amid a maze of beetles. But when a beetle really appeared, the metallic twang of his bass-viol flight removed all doubt. The millers pursued one another and flitted about like the ghosts of butterflies. Now and then they alighted on the dead leaves and made remarkably loud rustlings as they walked about.

At five o'clock the buzz of a fly was heard,—a sound wholly unlike the subdued owl-winged humming,—and at this tiny trumpet of day the night ended. As at the crow of the cock in the Danse Macabre, every little ghost scuttled to shelter, and then I looked up and realized that no longer were my eyes straining for vision. The comet had dimmed to the merest etching of light. Several birds broke into song. A pheasant crowed far up the mountain side, and two kaleege challenged below me. A partridge joined in, calling twice. The comet vanished; the East became a blaze of glory, blue and gold streaming over the mountains of Kashmir. A new day had broken in the Hills.

No more than twenty-four hours had passed when those gods were kind who are especially in attendance upon one who seeks to know the intimacies of pheasants. I knew the great tragopan of the western Himalayas was hereabouts—I had heard its strange mammal-like yowl, and I had shot a single male with gorgeous lappet wattle in full development. It was an undeserved snapshot for the bird had burst unexpectedly from behind a boulder on a hillside. Almost instinctively, I let off one of my three barrels from my hip, and secured the bird with a single pellet through the brain. It fell hundreds of feet down the brushy slope, and only the doglike senses of my Hillman ever located and retrieved it. I had to scream and yell at him, for as he made his way leisurely up the steep hill he casually pulled out one tail feather after another, a sort of avian "he loves me, he loves me not." There was no alternative in my mind, however, and with every plucked feather the Hillman was storing up trouble with me. I finally stopped him and to his disgust made him descend again and pick up the discarded plumes. He got every one and I reconstructed the tail of my prize. Pheasants and food were the only logical rhyme in my Hillman's mind! The plumage of this tragopan is beautiful beyond most birds—orange and gold, brown and black, with a score of constella-

Valley of the Jumna, near Garhwal

Cattle treading out the grain

Spires of Fir and Spruce in the Western Himalayas

Here the great gray langur monkeys frolic, and feast on the eggs of impeyan pheasants; here

tragopans nest among the branches

tions of silver stars scattered over all, from neck to tail.

Not long after this my cup of joy was filled when, from my observation tent, I watched a cock for full ten minutes, within a few yards distance. But the aforesaid cup was to overflow. No actual proof of the nesting in trees of these gorgeous pheasants had been forthcoming, until I was fortunate enough to stumble upon circumstantial evidence of so positive a nature that I include it in detail without hesitation. In this, as in my account of the roosting bird, the tragopan entered upon the scene wholly unexpectedly.

How often it is that Nature will suddenly exhibit to us a hint of some long-desired mystery when we least expect it, when perhaps we are wholly absorbed in something else—an unexpected gleam into the tail of our eye—and yet day after day, when we do our utmost to penetrate her secrets, she holds herself aloof and sphinx-like.

In this same range of native Garhwal on the border of Kashmir, I had set up my observation tent on a sloping hillside of pine. I placed it under and within the dense sweeping branches of a young deodar, so that it made a formless mound of green, indistinguishable from the mass of dark needle foliage about it. Here I left it for three days, and then entered it one morning with the intention of observing more closely some cheer pheasants, which were accustomed to pass over this slope twice a day. An hour after I had begun my vigil,

I cut a new observation slit in the rear, for the
purpose of finding the author of a sweet, silvery
thread of warbling notes. A moment before, they
had been uttered within a foot of the tent, and
now I found the bird had flown to the short de-
pressed branches of a silver spruce, forty feet up,
and not far away. The activity of the little bird,
whatever it was, prevented my identifying it; but
in searching for it, I discovered a rough mass of
sticks, lodged close against the trunk, and partly
overhung and concealed by several of the silvery-
green needle-fans of this splendid conifer. I
marked it down as an object for examination when
I should leave the tent, and, after the usual few
minutes of exercise and massage within my little
green mound, by which alone I could compel my
aching limbs to endure the hours of cramped posture, I returned to my survey of the hillside.

Passing over many unimportant but interesting
bits of forest life which I observed on this memorable day, I at last caught a low, pheasant-like
chuckle, which made every nerve tingle like an
electric shock. It came from behind, and, as I had
been thus outflanked more than once by pheasants,
I peered out, but could see no sign of life. Then
the chuckle again and the quaver of needles, and
on the branch below the stick nest I saw a large
bird. Even then, tragopans were so far from my
mind that I stared in unrecognizing bewilderment.
Once more the low gurgling chuckle came, and
the bird walked unsteadily to the trunk and leaped

up to the nest itself. Then I realized that I was looking at a western tragopan hen, and a few days later I was to hear the self-same low chuckle given as the vesper song of a cock bird.

The tragopan, in her dull, mottled garb, was almost invisible as she stood motionless beside the nest in the shadow of the spruce foliage. Soon she began to crane her head and neck about, and, bending low down, busied herself in some way invisible from where I watched. At last she jumped down to the branch below, then to the next, and so on, making a complete circuit of the trunk as she descended, and finally, when out of my sight, flew with but a low rustle of wings to the ground. For forty minutes I saw or heard nothing more, and then the crackle of a twig set me on the *qui vive,* and I soon saw her near the nest. A rough spruce twig had caught in her breast plumage and snapped off, tweaking out a feather or two, as I discovered when later I climbed the tree. Again she wrought silently at the nest, and again descended her resinous stairway. Once more she returned, this time with a beakful of leaves, which I could distinctly see, as they were so unlike the needles through which she ascended. She soon went away as before, and I never saw her again, although I waited until late afternoon, when my abused body would allow no further insult, and for very agony I had to leave my shelter and roll about upon the turf outside. Once having thrown caution to the winds, I climbed the tree with some difficulty, for the needle-armored, stiff-twigged maze made anything but pleasant going. Knowing that the wary bird would easily detect my clumsy trail of sap-bleeding footprints, I tied together the entire nest, brought it down, and made a careful analysis of the structure. A glance showed that it was not the work of the pheasant, but an old nest of some other bird; this disappointing fact being only too evident from the weather-worn character of the well-woven substructure of sticks and bleached grass. The lining was as obviously of very recent date; indeed, the green leaves of oak and some unknown weeds were still almost fresh and unwilted, while the twigs— a dozen or more with a strong aromatic scent, were still sappy at the end, for all had been freshly broken off, and none were dead or dried. All had been plucked within forty-eight hours, as I satisfied myself by actual comparison with leaves and twigs which I gathered one day and examined on the following. This was the work of the tragopan which I had been watching, although she could not have brought all the twigs and leaves on the three trips when under my observation. She must have begun work on the previous day.

I now turned my attention to the nest proper. I found that the twigs and grass were not nearly so bleached as the old dried stems about me on the ground, and traces of green near the nodes of the grasses seemed to make certain that it was this year's nest. Two small fragments of shell, which had sifted down into the matted lining, might have been parts of the egg of a raven or crow, or of many another species; it was impossible to make certain. The general character of the nest was corvine—no more could be said.

One can readily see how many terrestrial dangers would be avoided by birds of this size nesting in trees; but, on the other hand, if they are in the habit of utilizing the large stick nests built and already used by other birds, they are running considerably more risk than if they built a nest themselves. The nest of which I have written was remarkably well concealed. If I had not been close to the ground, and slightly down along the slope, I should never have discovered it. It was invisible when at last I stood up and looked toward it. But most used nests are much more in view. Constant approach of the parent birds breaks or wears away the adjacent leaves and twigs, and by the time the brood of the rightful owners is ready to leave, the nest is far from well concealed. Again, one hardly knows what nests could serve. In this instance the nest was doubtfully corvine, but such fearless, pugnacious birds usually build in plain view, a site which would give a hen tragopan but short shrift. The greatest danger attendant on arboreal nesting would be the Himalayan langur monkeys, and the betrayal to eagles by inquisitive crows and jays. That the monkeys are at times a very real danger to pheasant nests I well knew from my experience with the impeyan.

Three days later I again disarranged my khansamah's plans for a comfortably late, slowly served
breakfast. From the mess ground, both he and
the chowkidar gave forth intermittent discontented
rumbles, which died away as they approached the
camp table. This morning, however, it was only
for five o'clock that I demanded *chota hazri*.

As I trudged off with gun and glasses, I saw a
gray wraith disappear in the opposite direction,
and knew that Hadzia had started on his day's
hunt for the nest which was to bring him eight
rupees. Two days of disappointment had passed,
and his chagrin was so great that, if possible I
would gladly have "salted" a find for him with a
scraped-out depression and four brown-stained
hen's eggs. But this day was to be fortunate for
both of us: the pheasant star was in the ascendant.
Perhaps to this hour Hadzia recounts to his children the madness of Beebe Sahib which took the
form of paying out real money for useless eggs
and such baubles.

I walked quickly, for I knew my ground, and
climbing five or six hundred feet, reached the ridge
breathless, but before the sun rose. Keeping well
hidden on the nearer side, I crept several hundred
yards farther on, and, in the swiftly strengthening
dawn light, slipped through a boulder scar to my
chosen hiding place between an outjutting mass of
rocks and two ancient deodars. Beneath me were
spruce, fir, deodars, and oaks rising straight as
plummets from the steep slope. Every few yards

the trees thinned out into open, park-like vistas, carpeted with smooth natural lawns. In one place the grass was starred with myriads of purple and white anemones, but the dominant blossoms were long-stemmed strawberries which grew eight to the foot for acres. I had hardly settled myself and swiveled my glasses to sweep the field ahead when tragedy descended. With a swish of wings which rose to a roar as they passed, an eagle dropped from nowhere, seized some small creature, and with hardly a pause launched out over the valley and out of sight. The tip of a great pinion brushed a shower of dew from a spruce branch as the bird labored outward, and I found myself staring at swaying needles and wondering whether what had passed was reality or a vision. Hardly had the branch settled to rest than a small green warbler flew to it and chanted an absurdly confident ditty. The unconsciousness of the diminutive feathered creature increased the unreality of the tremendously dynamic display of power a second before.

As I mused on this startling introduction to the day's observation, the narrowness of us humans came to mind more vividly than ever. With such antitheses to stir the most sluggish blood, how can any real lover of nature and the wilderness of earth fail to react? My wonder is not with mediocre work. Many of us can never hope to reach the clear heights of quick dynamic thought, and the genius of generalization which in the last analysis is the only *raison d'être* of facts and the search for facts. Most of us must be content to gather the bricks and beams and tiles in readiness for the great architect who shall use them, making them fulfill their destiny if only in rejection. But I marvel that men can spend whole lives in studying the life of the planet, watching its creatures run the gamut from love to hate, bravery to fear, success to failure, life to death, and not at least be greatly moved by the extremes possible to our own existences. Why should science dull our reaction to the theme of "Louise"? Why should technicalities dry the emotion when a master makes Beau Brummel live again? Why should palaeontology or taxonomy detract a whit from "McAndrew's Hymn" or "the Jabberwocky"? Must sagittal sections and diagrams ever deaden one's appreciation of Böcklin and Rodin? Why should a geologist on a ballroom floor, or a botanist in the front row of a light-opera audience be considered worthy objects of abstract humor, instead of evincing a corresponding breadth of real humanness? Is it inevitable that occipital condyles and operas, parietals and poetry, squamosals and sculpture must be beloved by different individuals?

But the end of the minute's mood which conceived these wild thoughts brought me back to my perch among the deodars, and, like an apt moral, to another antithesis, a tragedy at my finger-tips among the infinitely small. Along the half-decayed bark of a tree fallen across the front of my hiding-place, a huge slug made its way. All unknown to me, this slug was a stranger to scientific mankind, and in the course of time he was to be examined half-way round the world by one learned in the structure of slugs, and to be christened with the name of his discoverer. But we were both wholly unconscious of this present lack and impending honor, quite as much as the race of *Anadenus beebei* is still happy in its ignorance of our altered godfatheral relations.

The great mollusk crept along the damp bark, leaving a broad shining wake of mucus, then tacked slowly and made its way back. In the meantime various creatures, several flies and spiders and two wood-roaches, had sought to cross or alight on the sticky trail and had been caught. Down upon them bore the giant slug and, inevitable as fate, reached and crushed them, sucking down the unfortunates beneath its leaden sides, its four, eyed tentacles playing horribly all the while. The whole performance was so slow and certain, the slug so hideous, and my close view so lacking in perspective, that the sensation was of creatures of much larger size being slaughtered.

The comparison of this lowly tragedy of slime with the terrific rush and attack of the eagle from out of the heart of the sky tempted one to thoughts even more weird than I have expressed.

But fortunately the actors for whose arrival I had been waiting now began to appear, and I longed for each minute to be an hour.

PHEASANT JUNGLES

We think of a hummingbird as quite the most brilliant and colorful creature in the world—a strange little being with the activity and bulk of an insect, the brain of a bird, and the beauty of an opal. Imagine one of these, shorn of its great activity but enlarged many times, and one has an impeyan pheasant of the Himalayas. Beneath, it is black as jet; its crest is a score of feather jewels trembling at the extremity of slender bare stalks. But its cloak of shimmering metal is beyond description, for with each change of light the colors shift and change.

When the· shadow of a cloud slips along the mountain slope the impeyan glows dully—its gold is tempered, its copper cooled, its emerald hues veneered to a pastel of iridescence. But when the clear sun again shines, the white light is shattered on the impeyan's plumage into a prismatic burst of color.

My eye caught a trembling among the maidenhair fern, and I swung my glass and brought a full-plumaged impeyan into the field. The dew and the soft light of early dawn deadened his wonderful coat. His clear brown eyes flashed here and there as he plucked the heads of tiny flowers from among the grass.

For fifteen minutes nothing more happened; then for the space of an hour impeyans began to appear singly or in pairs, and once three together. Finally fourteen birds, all cocks in full plumage, were assembled. They gathered in a large glade which already showed signs of former work, and there dug industriously, searching for grubs and succulent tubers. They never scratched like common fowl, but always picked, picked with their strong beaks. Every three or four seconds they stood erect, glanced quickly about, and then carefully scanned the whole sky. It was easy to divine the source of their chief fear—the great black eagles which float miles high like motes. The glittering assemblage fed silently, now and then uttering a subdued guttural chuckle.

When the sun's rays reached the glade, the scene was unforgettable: fourteen moving, shifting mirrors of blue, emerald, violet, purple, and now and then a flash of white, set in the background of green turf and black, newly upturned loam.

After the impeyans had been feeding for half an hour there arose a sudden excitement. Several disappeared among the surrounding deodars, and all stood listening and watching. Then feeding began in a desultory way, and one by one the birds left the glade until only two remained. My agony of body asserted itself, and with a groan of relief I stretched my cramped limbs—and in doing so shook a branch. At the instant both birds rose with a whirr, soared out over the top of the spruces, and gradually melted from view in the mists of the lower valley. To the last they shone like gems.

This company of birds had come from all directions and were all cocks. Their mates were brooding, hidden on a dozen slopes. Clad in their brilliant plumage, these cocks did not dare approach the nests, but roosted and lived apart. Early each morning they foregathered here for a silent feast in company, friendly with sheathed spurs, to separate after a little while and spend the remainder of the day by themselves, wandering among the magnificent deodars and over the glades of strawberry blossoms.

I had told no one of my destination that morning, and when I peered over the crest of the ridge I was surprised to see a man huddled close to the ground a few hundred feet down the slope. My glasses showed Hadzia sitting quietly, but not asleep. I could not easily return to camp without coming within his field of vision. As he had apparently trailed me, I amused myself by turning the tables, and backing away I crossed the crest farther on, slipping at once into a grove of young deodars. With care I stalked the pitiful bunch of rags, keeping trunk after trunk between us, and crawling on the ground over the one open space which separated us. The last fifty feet was easy, the slope gentle, trees convenient, the carpet of needles soft and deep. In a few moments I had reached the tree at his back and heard a low, minor chanting. Ten feet away it was inaudible; it was full of sorrow, of the tragic cadences of all savage music, yet I found it was Hadzia's hymn of victory.

The moment I stepped from behind the tree I was sorry I had played my little joke. He did

Hadzia – the Hillboy who Dared to Serve a Sahib

Hail-storm in Garhwal

All living things exposed to its force were killed

Nest and Eggs of Himalayan Nutcracker

This home was saved from the hail by the overhanging bank

what only the lowest savage does. His whole instinct was flight. There was no reflex reaching for a weapon, or the place where one might carry a weapon. Just sudden hopeless terror, and a rabbit-like bound. Nor was this followed by laughter as it should have been. The fear in his eyes was replaced by wonder, helpless, striving to understand. Then emotion of another sort returned, and shyly coming toward me, he reached into the folds of his garment—coarse, ragged, and as storm-stained as the century-old forest debris about him. Then across his face flitted a new expression. No words fitted it. When I had so thoughtlessly frightened him, his fear seemed to be a racial thing—a terror fostered through generations by threatened death from men and animals. It was impersonal and pitiful because it seemed to lay bare all lack of racial manliness. Where a Ghurka would have reached instinctively for his kokri, or a Dyak for his spear or my throat, the Hillman fled.

But now the hopelessness which marked his eyes as he watched my face was very different. This was not Hillmen's but Hadzia's sorrow, and the whole became clear as his grimy fingers came forth stained yellow, and with bits of clinging shell which I knew at once. He had found the nest of an impeyan.

The tragedy was complete. He had told my servant that he could remain only one more day. Two had been wasted, and now, early on the third, success had been attained. By some keen sensing he had followed my track, had not disturbed the Sahib at his inexplicable work, but doglike had crouched where he would intercept him on his return. Here he had waited, thinking no one knows what thoughts, and now at a whim of the Sahib's —a cruel, meaningless joke—the pheasant's eggs had been crushed.

Strong emotion has no lasting place in a Hillman's mind, and with a single shake to clear the yolk from his hand, Hadzia turned toward the camp, with exactly the same expression as when he had first appeared with his fellow hillmen. I was sorry for my lack of words, but led hastily to camp, where I summoned my khansamah and bade him thank Hadzia, pay over the eight rupees at once, and ask him to lead me to the nest. When Hadzia heard the harangue in which my comic khansamah always clothed my simplest sentences, he turned to me and opened his mouth, and for an instant I thought I saw a spark of real emotion in his brown eyes. But that too passed at once, and he took the coins, and placed them apparently in what must have been a pheasant omelette. He turned away a few steps and waited with the patience of which he was such a complete master.

This episode with Hadzia was a link in the chain to ultimate good fortune, coming when I was on my way to revisit and photograph his empty nest. I sank among a growth of tall ferns to watch a tiny crested tit carrying beakfuls of caterpillars to her brood in a hollow stub. Trip after trip she made, gleaning from low shrubs. Finally I heard her utter a scolding note and pause in her search. She concentrated her attention on a tangle of ivy, and had, I supposed, discovered a snake or some other creature worthy of her vocal contempt. I carefully focussed on the spot and saw my first brooding impeyan. To get a good view I had to climb up a half-dead spruce, and there I studied every web of her mottled plumage. The whole landscape seemed changed. Instead of an indefinite forest with varied interests, all was now centred about this spot—the home of the most beautiful of the pheasants. Just beyond in an open growth of oaks the underbrush was bright with roses and gracefully sweeping, pink-flowered raspberries; lower down under the denser foliage of the deodars were flowers of the shadows, growing singly or in friendly groups of several,—lilies-of-the-valley and Solomon's seal, or so they appeared to American eyes. Then as a closer setting to the nest were banks upon banks of maidenhair fern, all in deep shadow—a filmy tracery bending to breaths of air which I could not sense. And wherever the ferns failed, crept the ivy, winding its dull green trail over fallen trunks or seeking to hide every stump or half-dead tree.

For two days I watched from a distance, and at discreet intervals. In the absence of the mother, I examined the two amber shells and photographed them. Then late one afternoon as I passed by after a day with koklass pheasants, I saw tragedy, swift and sure, descend upon the impeyan home.

The crash and roar of a troop of langur monkeys came to my ears. As I approached, the noise lessened and died away in the distance; but as I came over the ridge, a long-tailed gray form leaped from the undergrowth upon a bare, half-fallen tree and ran along it on three legs, holding something clutched in one hand. I suspected trouble and ran headlong at the monkey, who promptly dropped his booty and fled off through the trees, swearing roundly at me the while. The nest was empty, and one egg in sight had a gaping hole in the side from which the yolk streamed.

Then the marauding monkeys swung past, old and young hurling themselves recklessly from spire to spire. Tree after tree shook and bent as in a terrific gale of wind; branches crashed and splintered; cones, needles, and twigs rained to the ground as the troop rushed by. The uproar which the bandarlog creates has usually but little effect upon the lesser creatures of the forest. They well know the danger and the limitations of the four-handed folk.

When this troop passed from view, however, quiet did not settle down. There was no wind, no movement of the needles; even the ferns hung motionless. But there was a sinister undercurrent of sound more potent than noise of elements. Something was about to happen, and not concerning any one animal, or in any one glade. The birds

1.   Satyr Tragopan in display

2.   Red Jungle Fowl

were restless and their notes were those of anxiety; small creatures dashed here and there among the leaves. Without knowing why, I picked up my gun and walked hastily toward camp.

I crossed two ridges. Still no wind, but still a sound of restless life everywhere, a tense uneasiness. And then came the climax. From the distant snows billowed a breath of cold air,—icy, unfriendly,—and at the shock the sun hid his face. A dark mist closed down. The forest creatures became silent as death, and for as long as two minutes the silence was oppressive. Then in the distance the trees bent and straightened, the mist yellowed and a drop of rain fell. Finally came a sound as strange as any in the world, the noise of ice falling on flowers and leaves, a mitrailleuse-volley of hail such as only the great Himalayas know. It was a repetition, only more severe, of the Sikhun hail storm.

Lashed by the ice, our horses whinnied with pain and fright, and although wild mountain ponies, crowded close to us beneath the shelter of the dâk. They pushed in out of the downpour, and while they had been exposed only to the first, rather light fall, yet their coats were covered with welts as if from blows of finely divided thongs of a whip.

After fifteen minutes of hail such as we are familiar with in the States, the stones grew larger and the downpour more furious, until the crash of falling ice dominated all other sounds. The floor of the valley became white and the hail-stones—now much larger than marbles—bounced and leaped high after their impact with the ground. I took several photographs which showed this, together with the flattening of the vegetation. Leaves and whole fans of spruce needles were torn away and covered the bruised blossoms of the forest slopes. The air was a screen of straight lines, breaking near the ground into a maze of dancing, splintering crystal balls.

Before the bombardment ended I put out my hand, with the result that one stone struck my thumb and lamed it for three days. Without warning the sun came out and made of the storm a translucent tapestry, through which the broken foliage was dimly visible. It was so wonderful, so unlike anything I had ever seen, that I forgot momentarily the terrible damage—the shredded foliage, the host of stricken nestlings and creatures which had not found a safe retreat. When the last missile had fallen I wondered whether the most hardy tenant of the forest had survived. And Nature in mockery at my ignorance, having ceased her cruel torrent, sent out the frailest of frail butterflies, flickering its copper wings before me in the sun.

I found others which had not been so fortunate, and in one spot beneath a thin-leaved bush were thirty-eight good-sized butterflies all of the same species, with wings only slightly torn, but all killed and partly buried beneath a mass of jellied hailstones. About fifty percent of the nests which I had under observation were destroyed, but some were preserved by overhanging banks. This was the case with a very beautiful babbler's nest, which, with its three eggs, was quite unharmed, sheltered in a niche in the side of a steep grassy bank.

Not far away, behind a bit of loosened deodar bark, was a most delicate nest of a rufous-capped titmouse, with three dead and one unharmed young bird. Two big hail-stones had crashed down, one being wedged a few inches above the nest, while the other had fallen with full force into the mass of moss and pheasant feathers, and then slipped over the edge. The forlorn youngster, balancing himself on a bit of stick, looked as if life held out no hope of any kind, but at the chirp of his parents, who had miraculously escaped, he opened his eyes, and when I left him after taking his picture, he had his mouth wide agape, begging as only infant birds can.

I found traces of many other tragedies, one of the most unexpected being the bodies of two giant flying squirrels. These splendid rodents which weighed as much as five pounds, and are over three feet in length, are not uncommonly seen in the dusk of evening volplaning from trunk to trunk in these mighty evergreen forests, as I had seen them at midnight in the light of the comet. These had apparently been sleeping in a half-hollowed-out space behind some bark which had been torn away, and the ice had stunned and killed them before they could escape. Lizards were flattened on rocks and logs, and the total de-struction of animal life must have been very great. Certainly no creature of small size had any chance if exposed to the full fury of the ice. A chicken in an open crate was so injured that we had to kill it.

Taken altogether, this Kashmir storm was the most sudden and severe one I have ever witnessed, and my servants would have had a bad time of it if they had not been able to reinforce the sloping walls of their tent and so keep them under cover. As it was, great rents were torn in the canvas and the men were pretty badly frightened by the time it was all over.

On the last day of my stay in Garhwal I squatted native-fashion on a steep slope, watching the day slowly die, and stirred as I always am with the great desire to remain: So quickly had this iso-lated valley become home, so familiar had its trails become, yet so few of its secrets had I been able to solve. Always its great age had impressed me, its centuries-old deodars, the soaring lammergeiers which seemed never to have known youth. But now a new sound—in this land of strange sounds —came to me: a rhythmic beat, beat, too mechan-ical, too regular to be elemental. It was dull, muf-fled, and seemed very far off. But this was an il-lusion, for almost at once four men swung into view around a curve in the trail, and four others, and still four and four. My pulse leaped as a whole company of British regulars filed before me and broke ranks near my camp. What a contrast to the ragged Tibetans and Hillmen who for centuries had preceded them and for many years would follow! The spell of the wilderness was broken. My last link had been my thoughts aroused by the rhythm of the comet. Hadzia had fitted into the scheme of detachment here, as if he had been a faun or satyr. Now my connection with the outside world was forged anew by the rhythm of these men.

That evening as I sat on the hillside with a group of officers and listened to the soldiers' concert, the cockney accent in story and song fell on my ears like something recurring from a distant alien memory. I was glad to know that the pheasants and Hadzia had so profoundly influenced me.

When the camp-fire had burned to embers, and I had bade goodnight to the last of my officer hosts, I walked slowly up toward camp. Beyond the ridge I heard yet a new sound, yet a new rhythm, and my heart warmed to the sight. Around a flicker of twig-embers squatted the white forms of four natives—my khansamah and three soldiers' servants. Two had battered tin pans and sticks, and to the tom-tom beat their voices chanted some sad, minor melody, as old, probably, as India is old. I glanced up at the faint glow of the receding comet, and I thought of Hadzia somewhere deep among the distant mountains, perhaps with his hand close about his eight rupees—rupees whose brightness was dimmed with the yolk which had gained them. For the moment I resented the intrusion of those splendid rhythmic men. I wondered what Hadzia's thoughts might be. And I knew that if they were filled with affection for these Hills and a great yearning never to leave them, they were mine also.

IV

ONE of my earliest and most cruel disillusionments came during a season of grammar school wrestling with geography, when I left my pink natal state of New York and, in the course of a short trip discovered to my disgust that New Jersey was not blue, nor Pennsylvania even scarlet. When I re-adjusted my mind to this hopeless lack of political soil differentiation, I still retained an interest in boundaries and frontiers and with the years and the miles this has increased instead of lessening. So when I set my face northward from Rangoon and saw on the map the tiny village of Ta-So almost on the exact meeting place of Burma, Tibet and China, I intended that my pheasant trailing should lead thither.

From Rangoon to Mandalay the train hurried me along through three hundred miles of rice-fields, all like great lakes after the recent rainy season. Pond herons, egrets, marabou storks and sarus cranes stood statuesquely about looking at their reflections in the paddy pools; the telegraph wires were dotted with dusky drongos, azure rollers and emerald bee-eaters; the number and tameness of the birds eloquently proclaiming the ancient and

97

benign faith of the Buddha to be more potent than our modern societies for the preservation of birds, for the true Buddhist holds sacred all life, even the smallest and meanest.

The train deposited its burden of chattering tourists at Mandalay, all those who had "done" Rangoon, and were now girding up their dusters to "do" Mandalay in the brief, exact time allotted in their dizzy whirl around the world. With no hurrying West on its mind the train for Upper Burma more leisurely traversed three hundred and fifty miles farther into the interior of Asia, and gently dropped me at Myitkyina, the end of all railway travel, and the champion word to offer conceited linguists for correct pronunciation,— *mitch-i-nah* is as near as I can write it. The Burma of gilded pagodas and temples, of dainty, silk-clad maidens—the Burma of superlatively gorgeous oriental color—was many miles behind me; before lay Upper Burma, Yunnan and Tibet, a wilderness of lonely mountains, sparsely peopled with wild hill folk.

For the night, food and shelter were the immediate problems, while on the morrow there was the matter of outfit for the coming trip into the wilderness. I knew that Myitkyina boasted nothing so ambitious as a hotel, but I had sent Aladdin on ahead with government chits of introduction and I knew he would not fail me. I hailed a gharry and got into it, shouting, *Dâk! jeldhi! jeldhi! Dâk!* to the ancient driver. To all accredited travellers the

Our Elephant on the Trail near Pongatong in Northern Burma

The Valley of Tragedies

My camp in the heart of Sansi Gorge, on the border between Burma and China

word dâk conveys often a meaning no less than home, although these government rest-houses are mere empty rooms, it being taken for granted that bedding, food and servants are being brought by the occupant.

But my mind was taken off the prospective dâk by the present gharry. A gharry is ramshackle when it is made; primary usage in Calcutta removes any comfortable qualities it may have possessed. It is then condemned and shipped to Rangoon where it is tied together and used with patience and enthusiasm. A time comes when the gharry patrons of Rangoon refuse further to trust their lives within it, and then it is sent north. At Myitkyina I discovered the final port of gharries, the spot where they are made to yield the last few minutes of transportation before dissolution into original elements. Twice we stopped en route; once when a war-bag fell through the floor and was run over, and another time when the driver came to a halt for some reason of his own, perhaps to pray. Rocking and jouncing along, my head bouncing against the skeleton top like a grain of corn in a popper, we reached the dâk.

There, on the verandah, standing guard over a pile of my possessions was a long, lean, swarthy native, with the most scowling, villainous face I have ever seen. On top of the face was a bright, scarlet fez. I was about to throw him out when Aladdin dashed around the corner, out of breath, salaaming profoundly. Associating the stranger with one of the horrible genie of the Arabian Nights, I was about to ask Aladdin "Where is the lamp?", but substituted, "Where on earth did you get him?"

"Oh, Marster," said Aladdin carelessly, "I meet on train coming. I tell about you. He like cook for us. He Mohammet." The thought of setting out after species of the genus *Gennæus* and perhaps *Chrysolophus* with both Aladdin and Mohammed in my entourage was too good to worry about, so I accepted him on the spot. As a matter of fact his murderous expression never changed by day or night through all the coming weeks; he would tramp along a muddy road for half a day with a bundle of cross-bow loot without a murmur, and he would squat for hours on end before his cooking pots in the heart of camp,—but through it all he forever scowled and scowled. However, his waffles were perfect, as we may presume his collops would be had he known anything about them, and neither Aladdin nor he had claimed anything for his character.

Before I went to sleep that first night I went into the compound and looked across the Irrawaddy River to the dim, distant hills and as usual, had a fit of pessimistic terror at my presumption in planning to penetrate deep into this strange wilderness with so little knowledge of its dangers, whether of animals or of men, and wondered whether I had not better take the train back to Rangoon next day. I always go through this stage on the eve of any new undertaking, and while it lasts it is very real and very terrible. But somehow I always manage to stick it out and it passes with the first good night's sleep, or the first danger overcome.

I found my usual difficulties multiplied many-fold, for Myitkyina was at this time a very active military outpost. Trouble was brewing on the Burma-Chinese border, and all mules were needed for a punitive column which the British government was about to send into the mountains. This fact was confided to me as a state secret, to explain why the officials wanted to dissuade me from making my trip just at this time. But I had come many thousands of miles, and time was precious. Even if I had to go with few carriers and live off the country I intended to try. And as my corpse might cause international complications the mules were promised on condition that I take a suitable guard with me.

Before daylight on a bitterly cold morning I was on the move with all my necessaries, and crossed the Great River at this point, seven hundred and fifty miles above where it empties into the Bay of Bengal. A reliable Chinese muleteer promised that sixteen mules, two horses, and men to care for them would follow in a few days. In the meantime I planned to stay at a little bungalow at Wain-Maw, just across the river, free from drilling regiments and nearer the pheasants. But preparations for war were still forwarder at Wain-Maw, so I arranged for another day's march by bullock cart. Our destination was Wah-hsaung, a tiny native village at the foot of the mountains. The rain began to fall in torrents, and in the leaky bungalow I waited patiently until three bullock carts arrived. The carts would not have been good bullock-carts on level ground, but here we traversed trails adapted rather for agile hillmen on foot. When one wheel rose three feet into the air, it was a nice question in physics and impetus and acceleration whether I and all my guns and ammunition and cameras would not be spilled down the hillside or into solid rock walls. Squeak, squeak, squeak—the native encourages his axles in squeaking, for everyone knows that thus are evil spirits frightened away from the trails. Huddled up under the tarpaulin, in the downpour, striving to ease the more delicate lenses and gun locks from the terrible jolting, I caught not a glimpse of this part of Upper Burma. There were only visible the enormous flat feet and the gaunt legs of my genie cook slopping through the mud after the cart. At Wah-hsaung after uncounted hours I crawled out and saw a white-washed bungalow with a diminutive chowkidar wrestling with a bunch of mighty keys.

For a week I lived here, waiting for the mule train, but I found several species of pheasants and could have kept busy at my scientific work for many months. On various sides of the dâk was an icy cold, rocky torrent, a dense forest, the trail into China, and, a hundred yards away, a small Shan village. This was the last of this tribe, for in the hills there were only Kachins. Whenever I visited the huts, all the inmates fled at top speed, leaving only several scores of snarling, half starved, pariah dogs to greet me.

The first quarter mile of forest was easy going, for it was threaded in all directions by the trails made by the semi-domesticated water buffalos, and by adapting one's height to that of a tall cow one could walk anywhere. The law of compensation was that whenever I met one of the buffalos themselves it was a question as to whether I could retreat quickly enough to avoid being charged. I got so that at certain times of the day I never failed to have some climbable tree spotted in the corner of my eye. Five times I had as narrow escapes as I have had from any wild animals in my life, and spent many hours up trees, waiting to be rescued by infant natives who would drive the great brutes away and allow me to come down. Once I had to kill an animal to save my camera and incidentally my life, for my perch was so precarious that the least push would have dislodged me.

Deeper in the jungle I could rely only on the half-burrowing trails of wild boars, and my anatomy is far from being porcine, in elevation at least. It was difficult country, and I had sometimes to caterpillar for hundreds of yards, through thorns and dense scrub. But my aches and pains were forgotten when at last I would come into sight of a cock pheasant and his harem, busily scratching for a living. Sometimes the prize was a glossy jungle-fowl, with drooping tail and red and gold ruff, or there would come into sight a flock of immaculate black and white silvers with scarlet wattled heads erect and on the alert. My heart would thump with excitement at this culmination of perhaps many hours' stalking, and I would watch them for a time with the glasses and then shoot what specimens I wished to use for study in the monograph.

The woods about Wah-hsaung were very lovely, beautifully draped with blossoming vines, musical with the cooing of spotted doves, while black-and-white as well as yellow wagtails lived up to their names with an eternal wagging as they scurried about the river bank. Blue-bearded bee-eaters, short-tailed green parrots and turquoise rollers were like glowing tropical blossoms which had taken unto themselves wings. A pygmy falcon lived here—only five inches long, but every inch a falcon—with a tiny, ferocious face, threatening eyes, beak of prey and minute but perfectly good talons.

My mule train arrived at last and in the midst of inconceivable confusion we started for the Chinese wilderness. In the darkness of early dawn the mules were unruly, the three Chinese mule-boys sleepy and stupid, Aladdin in frantic excitement shouting to them to hurry in a language of which they knew not a single word. With true Chinese indifference and dry humor they remarked to the chowkidar that the conversation of Aladdin reminded them of nothing so much as the barking of a dog, which speech was at once relayed to Aladdin who danced with rage, to the immense amusement of the China boys. From that day on it was open warfare between them and excitable little Aladdin, but as the conflict took the form of emulation in amount of work accomplished, I, like a bystander profiteer, derived only benefit from the mental battle, and, I am ashamed to say, occasionally fed the flames of competition. Meanwhile, above all the mêlée rose the braying of countless mules.

At last I decided to go on and leave the pack train to follow. Mohammed had appointed himself temporary syce and I found my saddle girthed to the horse's neck and both reins fastened on the same side of the bit. These mistakes, which cookie considered trivial, were set right and off I went with a Burmese boy as interpreter. To be sure he knew no English, but as cookie spoke a little Burmese, I hoped that ideas and sometimes facts might filter from me to Aladdin, thence through cook to the Burmese boy and possibly on to the Kachins.

For a few miles the trail led through level country and across a dashing little river, then we began the climb up to Pungatong, three thousand feet above us. The boy trudged on behind, a funny, picturesque figure. He was clad in a loose, short, white jacket, a kerchief of cerise silk about his neck and a sarong-like skirt of blue-and-green from hips to heels. His long black hair formed a psyche knot at the back of his head and he carried a huge parasol of orange paper, through which the light shone warm gold upon his face, which was that of a Burne-Jones lady done in sepia. From a distance Hurry Chunder Mookerjee could have called him brother.

The trail wound upward through utterly lovely country bathed in sunshine. We circled hills, sometimes descending for a time but always to rise higher on the next slope. A day's progress was like a strange slow motion picture of undulations in the sea of mountains. The bobbing parasol of our guide was now far behind. Hardly anywhere have I ever seen so many butterflies at one time, and of so many species. They swarmed in the sunshine like clouds of giant gnats, of every conceivable hue—like the throngs of gay, silk-clad Burmese maids who gather about the railway stations of Lower Burma. They carpeted the trail, fluttering up before our horses' hoofs, sometimes to alight upon us or the horses, or to drift off down the valleys. The Burman believes that butterflies are the spirits of human beings who are asleep, able at such time to go fluttering about the world at will. Thus only by accident will they kill a butterfly, or only for the gravest reasons will one Burman waken another, for his butterfly spirit may be wandering who knows where, and illness or death may come to him before the spirit has a chance to return. Fortunately most of my work lay above the zone of abundant butterflies, so my Burmese

The Village of Sin-Ma-How in Sansi Gorge

The Gracious Wife of the Headman of Sin-Ma-How

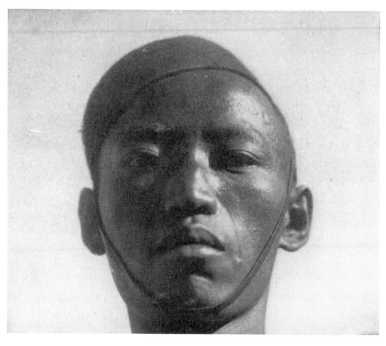

Number One Boy of My Gurkha Escort

lacked the constant suggestiveness for prolonged slumber.

When I reached the elevated bungalow at Pungatong I felt exhilarated and fit. Before the first night was over I knew the horrors of acute nervous breakdown. It is probable that only explorers will really comprehend what I mean, when waking fears and sleeping terrors combine to kill every enthusiasm and desire for work. The thought of going on was impossible. I hated pheasants, the jungle and all its inmates. For many months I had outfitted and carried on in most unhealthy regions and with the ever present worry that this or that species might escape my utmost efforts. The fact that I had had most astonishingly excellent luck seemed to matter not at all. The fact remained that at the auspicious beginning of this most important part of the expedition my only desire was to turn and run back to Rangoon, to America, to my home as fast as possible and never think pheasant again. This was a very different thing from the passing initial fears which prefaced each new phase of work. Physically I seemed fit, tonics were not indicated, I had no fever. I lit my candle lantern and roamed about the bungalow trying to estimate in how few days I could make my return. I even felt no shame at quitting; to quit, and to quit at once was all. I blundered into a small closet and as I opened the door I was deluged by piles of yellow-backs and penny dreadfuls which fell out upon me in disordered heaps.

PHEASANT JUNGLES

In a moment of curiosity I picked one up and read a chapter where the handsome hero choked a baboon, shot a murderous native and rescued the beautiful maiden, carrying her off through an underground tunnel which had been used by cavemen tens of thousands of years ago. On the walls of this cavern the two fugitives discovered prehistoric paintings of themselves, proving that they had been lovers in a former incarnation. I read on and on, stopping only to light new candles from the guttering end of the one before. Day came. I gave orders to camp here. Aladdin served breakfast and I snapped at him and cursed him when he waited for further orders. He crept fearfully forth in hurt wonderment, reporting an ill and irate Sahib. I read through the meal and on until I slept, then woke and continued. In short I lost count of the trash which I absorbed with breathless interest, and the following night I slept with hardly a dream. For two more days I read more fitfully, and at intervals even gazed without disgust at the distant line of blue mountains. When Aladdin timidly brought in the first trapped pheasant I identified it and measured it before I remembered my recently evolved hatred of them. Never again will I look wholly unmoved upon a yellow-backed novel or a penny dreadful.

At Pungatong I added silver pheasants and peacock pheasants to my note-books and collection of skins. In the jungle here brilliant wine- and chestnut-colored trogons swung from branch to branch, great hornbills flew overhead with a roar of wings like a rushing wind, pearl-gray monkeys watched me with never-quenched curiosity. One of my most unexpected finds came when I was stalking jungle-fowl. In the bed of a half-dried stream I saw unexpectedly a wallowing, mud-caked back and heard loud snortings. Mechanically I jumped for the nearest tree, and was just swinging myself up out of reach when the creature raised its head and instead of the low swung horns of a water buffalo I saw, to my astonishment, a long, upright unicorn—it was a huge rhinoceros, rare indeed at this latitude, and elevation of over half a mile.

During the few days of my mental convalescence at the dâk my interest gradually became transferred from heaven-sent trash to passing caravans,—unending lines of mules with tinkling bells and heavy loads, and Chinamen blue-clad, with queues twisted out of the way to give them greater freedom to cope with mule psychology. Rarely a Chinaman pompous and fat with material prosperity, rode past, sitting sideways on his mule, and looking about with that supreme condescension of one who rides while others walk.

Far more exciting were immense droves of hogs being urged along the trail—urged, but oh! how gently. One Chinaman walked in front keeping up a monotone of *Lulá! Lulá! Lulá!* Behind him came another Chinaman with a long stick persuasively pointing the way, while in the rear, others circled circumspectly to keep the restless army intact. In my weakened mental mood I saw worthy morals herein—an epitome of human nature, oppressive and overbearing where it dares to be, servile when it must. Everywhere in the world it is with shouts and oaths and blows that the long-suffering mule is made to do man's bidding, while to the hog man addresses himself in the most coaxing of tones. With such bromidic ideas finding lodgment in my mind I realized that my sanity had had a narrow escape indeed!

I was occasionally honored by officer guests, and Aladdin would meet me on my return from the jungle in wild excitement, sputtering the news that two hungry Englishmen had arrived without kits. "Think better ask to tiffin" counseled Aladdin, "Have got goosey-stew, junglefowl curry, sago pudding."

I remember few experiences more delightful than these chance meetings among the frontier hills of Burma. England sends of her best to look after her interests in her colonies, and the lives and adventures of many of these youngsters would make most fiction pall. When any of these officers spent the night at the bungalow, there was always a Gurkha soldier on guard. They looked very grave when they found that I was alone, with no escort. There was no telling what the hill people would do, let alone the cruel border tribes. The officers brought with them all the paraphernalia for heliographing, taking advantage of the autumn sunshine to send messages flashing all over northern Burma by means of native operators, to whom it was all cipher since they did not know a word of English. Now and then an English officer would be brought back by his servants and the Gurkhas on his way to Myitkyina, haggard and spent with fever in this brief time.

Through a forest of great, white, blossoming trees I reached Pumkan, where I found a microscopic dâk and a young lieutenant serving tea to himself under the blossoms. On I went, always higher and colder, and halted for a few days at Sadon, the jumping-off place, a little fort perched on a mountain top. Here imperative orders had been received from Viceroy headquarters, that I was on no account to be allowed to proceed without an armed escort of six Gurkhas. My retinue now numbered fourteen mules, three horses, three muleteers, cookie, Aladdin and the sextet in knee-trowsers, brown felt hats cocked up on one side, rifles and murderous kokris.

On and on I went, over villainous trails, and a loose log bridge which let one of our horses slip through. Fortunately I was not mounted at the time or my pheasant hunting would have come to an abrupt end. The horse could not go back and the mules could not follow. I sent back to find that the outfit had taken another route. The trail became a foot path, steep and rocky, with bamboos which whipped cruelly across my face. At three o'clock my way was blocked by a roaring torrent.

At five it would be bitterly cold, at six dark as midnight. I had no matches, and no food since morning. The night and another day must pass before I could retrace my steps. I went ahead to reconnoiter and encountered a wild-eyed Kachin armed with a cross-bow, who excitedly indicated that I was to follow. He took me around a bend in the river, but to do it I had to turn my horse into a mountain goat. At last I caught sight of a bit of paper shining in a cleft stick. It read,

"Turn to write."

It was from Aladdin, and assuredly he was in truth as well as etymologically a "Gift of God." The worst trail of all followed, when the poor horse crawled rather than walked up the mountain side. From the top a glorious view of three valleys was had, and on the summit of a half-bare hill I could make out my tents. Aladdin dancing up and down, and with his broadest and most toothless smile, greeted me with, "You find my chit? I give Kachin money to show me. More money to take chit. I fraid you in China by now."

Here I settled down for serious work and here I found more personality in a host of half-wild fellow humans than I usually experience on a whole expedition. Cookie and his strange character was completely forgotten amid scores of still more baffling men. Caucasian influence had given way to Mongolian mixtures. And wherever there is

Mongolian control there is also mystery and secrecy. Hidden motives lie behind the smallest trivalities of the day. Men pass by on the trail like shadows, and their faces tell nothing of what is in their hearts.

The whole country was in a state of upheaval and unrest. Along the border and beyond, marauding bands of Chinese and hybrid robbers were having things pretty much their own way. As I look back I can attribute my immunity from harm during the first half of my sojourn only to my complete ignorance of the actual conditions. When a stranger comes to a troubled country and goes about in jungle and over the mountains unattended, intent only on stalking wild birds, it would be natural for any enemies to think that this must be some kind of trap, and that he had adequate means of defence not visible to the naked eye. I learned later that throughout the entire region we were known to be the advance scouts of the column of the 96th Punjabis who, with elephants, were later to push forward their punitive column to our present position.

The Gurkhas had pitched camp on this hill-top for defensive purposes, with their own and those of the servants straggling down the side. Just beyond the dip of the valley was the semi-Chinese village of Sin-Ma-How, a dozen thatched huts set well back among trees, while at one side an icy torrent showed white against the green background. The valley stretched on and on toward

Tibet, and when the early morning clouds drifted down from the Yunnan mountains it was filled to the brim with dense blue vapor which, moving before a light wind, assumed a thousand forms and shadowy outlines.

As I came to know them, I developed greater interest and admiration for my Gurkhas. They were well-trained men, natural fighters, and the only mercenaries in the British army allowed to retain their native side-arms, the kokries—a compliment to their courageous little independent state. They were keenly interested in the shooting phase of my work, and as special favor I allowed them now and then to take a shot-gun and hunt pheasants. They were usually unsuccessful, but the excuses they offered were many. Monkeys and various creatures of goodly size were said to have been killed by mistake. And every day my guard would mourn over the stolid natives who would not fight. The persistent peace seemed somehow a reflection upon their function in the expedition, and they would have liked a modest battle on the doorsteps of each village. When my shot-gun disappeared into the underbrush, there was always a gambling chance that a luckless native would be suddenly and surreptitiously adjudged a pheasant. Therefore I was invariably relieved day after day to find monkeys the only primates in their bag.

In many countries there is a sharp line drawn between the master and the servant. Superiority and a corresponding inferiority are automatically

Night Guard at the Camp

Bamboo Rests for Nats or Evil Spirits

These were erected about the camp by superstitious natives

Lishao Woman with Baby

The elaborate decorations are in startling contrast with the filth and squalor of the owner's life

established by the relationship itself. In Burma this was not true. Every man in my camp was at my service at any hour of the day or night, but these men were of good caste. They were governed in all that they did by their own subtle, complex laws which no artificial conditions could destroy or overthrow.

The Gurkhas, of course, ate by themselves and from their own dishes. One day I thoughtlessly reached over their pot of rice for a crossbow which my syce held. Aladdin, close beside me, whispered, "Careful of rice, Marster." Then I remembered and drew back quickly. All of us laughed together and I went away, but I watched from my tent and saw them throw out the rice, which was polluted by the touch of my shadow. The pot itself was thoroughly cleansed. They would have to wait hours for the new rice to cook, and they were hungry and tired from a long march. But this mattered little when placed side by side with a spiritual scruple.

In this incident neither offense nor resentment played a part. It was simply the law and the law is sacred. Next day I bought a sheep and summoned the corporal to kill it in his own way that he and his men might share it. He saluted, smiled, and we became better friends. If superiority and inferiority entered into this, we divided them equally between us.

It was in this camp that I again formed my interpreting quartette. The members were myself, Aladdin, a Burmese, and a native Kachin, or whoever the fourth might chance to be. The results were weird and wonderful.

"Are there pheasants here?" I would ask.

"Snow come sometime," would be the answer.

One experience will suffice of the actual pheasant work. About three o'clock in the afternoon of one of my first days in this region, when the sun still held back the sting of the coming night air, I left camp with gun and glasses and climbed clear to the summit of the great eastern ridge. I stood actually on the divide which shunts its eastern waters into China and its western into the great rivers of Burma. Below me lay a mass of tumbled mountains and mighty valleys. All was forest, bamboo, oak and other hard woods, and it was on these slopes that I found kaleege pheasants which showed strains of silver, lineated and horsfields— one of the few instances in nature of the meeting and interbreeding of distinct species.

As I climbed I rejoiced to breathe deeply of this living vital air, after months spent in hot, steaming jungles. The sun went into a faint haze and the distant mountain peaks of Tibet changed to a deeper purple than ever painter dared put to canvas. At this hour the liquid chorus of bulbuls was the major theme with a minor accompaniment of booming doves.

I went swiftly down l ll and reaching the forest, turned into one of the old native trails. The ground was littered with dried leaves, and the wind soughing through the bamboos gave an added hint

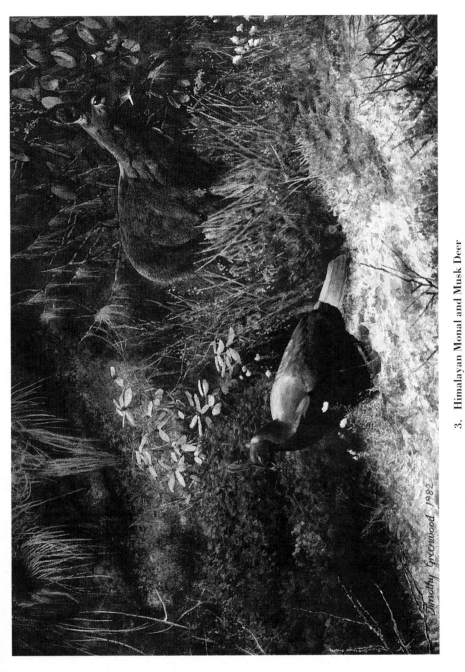

3. Himalayan Monal and Musk Deer

4. Western Tragopan

5. Reeves's Pheasant

6. Bulwer's Wattled Pheasant

of autumn even in this southern latitude. The rains were just over and the foliage was bright and clean. I crept as quietly as possible down to the very bottom of a deep ravine which the sun's rays had already left, for I knew that the pheasants were certain, sooner or later, to come down to this level for their evening drink. Near the low murmur of the rivulet I seated myself and began my vigil. For an hour I sat thus, making certain that the birds had not yet come down. Through the curtain of lofty ginger stalks overhead I could see drongos darting here and there after insects; small flycatchers and babblers passed in flocks, drinking and flitting upward again. Mosquitoes rose in clouds and pestered me sorely. Once the low tree-ferns on the opposite bank were shaken, and through the deeper shade of their fronds I saw a small tiger-cat passing, slowly, sinuously. He perhaps also knew that pheasants come here to drink.

Knowing from the silence that they were not yet among the bamboo above, I crept obliquely up the valley. Tree-vines hung their great masses of bloom overhead, and graceful wisteria-shaped flowers lightened the gloom with their pink and salmon petals, and spread far their musky odour—that of hemiptera. Some four-footed creature dashed from my path and, marking its fright, left another sharp stratum of musk upon the air.

I came upon a maze of footprints, where pheasants had that morning crossed the muddy rim of the pools, and here I turned directly upward. I know of no more difficult feat than attempting to climb noiselessly up a steep bank through clumps of bamboo, the ground covered with the driest of sheaths and leaves. I passed the grave of a Kachin chief, covered by an oval, thatched hut and a curious ornament of dyed bamboo. Just beyond I reached the mule trail, which at this point cut into the bank of the upper slope. Still hearing nothing, I climbed half-way to the summit of the ridge, here an open growth of oaks, when suddenly a shift in the breeze brought to my ears a loud scratching and rustling among the fallen leaves beyond the summit. I was exposed to full view, so with all possible speed I backed down the hill on hands and knees, crossed the trail and ensconced myself in a small thicket, which gave me full view of the slope which I had just left.

For half an hour I heard nothing, then a leaf flew upward from a tangle of vines, and a sturdy form leaped high over a log into view. It was not a pheasant, but a big, black-gorgeted laughing thrush. Another and another hopped down the slope, now hidden by tree-trunks or bushes, now standing out in full silhouette. There were sixteen in all, spread out in a segment of a circle, and chuckling low to themselves at every succulent morsel. They are splendid, sturdy birds, jay-like from beak to claw, now holding a wormy acorn and pounding away as hard as a woodpecker, then, ant-thrush-like, picking up leaves and throwing them far over their backs. I was absorbed in

118

watching their gradual approach when a jungle-fowl crowed loudly in the valley beyond the ridge, and brought my mind sharply back to pheasants. I was keenly disappointed at having apparently missed my birds, and half rose to go. At my first motion a laughing thrush set up a truly jay-like yell, and answers came from a score of throats, guffaws and peals of loud laughter which no real jay could ever produce. I sat quiet, their alarm passed, and they began to sail overhead down the valley. Not being certain at this time of the species I fired and secured one.

I waited five minutes and heard not a sound, save the calls of the laughing thrushes far down below me. Rising stiffly, and slowly moving out into the trail, I began to reload, when halfway up the slope a black head and neck shot up, and the warning or suspicion cry of a kaleege pheasant rang out sharp and shrill.

I dropped flat upon the trail, and caterpillared back over the edge into my thicket again. Not a cluck or call came from the slope above but little by little a low sub-sound of rustling leaves, and in ten minutes the ground over which the laughing thrushes had passed was being quartered by eleven splendid pheasants. With balanced glasses I could see every feather. Four were adult cocks, four were hens, while the other three were nearly grown young males. Without doubt four of them comprised a still united family of the present year, while five others seemed to represent another. To my surprise I could easily distinguish between three of the male birds. A solitary cock was the lightest of all, one of the young males appeared as dark as a black-breasted kaleege, while its brother was lightly vermiculated. I watched the dainty birds stepping high like thoroughbreds, snatching an insect or leaping at some morsel on a leaf overhead, or picking up an acorn, ever alert and watchful. I remained as still as the tree-trunk at my back, and the birds descended half-way down the slope toward me.

Then two Kachin women, with silver cylinders and tassels in their ears, and great baskets on their backs, came along chattering loudly. They halted when they saw me, and despite all my motions stood stupidly gaping at me for several minutes before they plodded on their way. The pheasants had, of course, retreated to cover, and when, twenty minutes later, they returned they were spread out more irregularly. I secured the light-colored old male, which I had seen the day before, and three others, while the rest passed me on either hand, together with a junglecock, which in bearing and gait was not to be compared with the far more elegant and graceful pheasants. Except for a short, sharp alarm note and five minutes of silence, the flock paid no attention to the roar of my gun. As I had opportunity to notice on many other occasions, if one shoots from a thicket and makes no movement after firing, the birds seem to have no sense of direction of the danger and are but little

A Woman of Sin-Ma-How with Enormous Ear-bars of Silver

A Strange Tribesman Visiting my Camp

Within a week and less than a mile away he was killed, probably by leopards. Aladdin in the offing

affected by the sight of their dead companions. When headed down toward water I have never known a flock to be turned back by shots fired in this way, and have secured as many as seven valuable specimens from the same ambush.

The few crickets whose instruments were not yet silenced by the autumn chill, still shrilled as I retrieved my game. Small owls hawked about after droning beetles; a podargus fanned my cheek like the ghost of a bird, and far off in the blackness, from the direction of the Chinese mountains, came the moan of a leopard. As I turned campward, a wind—first prophet of tomorrow's storm—rattled the bamboos, drawing forth weird sounds which seemed to verify the Kachin's belief in the spirit *nats* which wander along every trail at night searching for evil to do. For this reason these wild hillmen will never travel far at night, and as I trudged toward camp, I knew that whatever dangers the darkness hid at that hour were from animal and not human foes.

For a time I thought that the inhabitants of Sin-Ma-How had determined obstinately to ignore the strange household which had sprung up so suddenly on the opposite hill. But the second morning when I opened the flaps of my tent I saw a mushroom growth of *nat* rests clustered together at one side. These were little openwork frames and cones of interlaced cane, perched on low bamboo poles. Superficially they might be a topsy-turvy forest of music racks, deserted in wild confusion by the sudden flight of some insane orchestra. Functionally they afforded adequate resting places for the evil *nat* spirits with which our camp was supposed to abound; by resting on these they were propitiated and lulled into forgetting their sinister witchcraft. The approach of the natives the preceding night had not escaped the vigilant eyes of my Nepalese sentry, but while he despised these hybrid tribes of this no-man's-land, yet he respected religious customs and discreetly looked the other way while they planted their little propitiatory chaises-longues. When at dawn I saw the bamboo baskets I acquired merit with my Babelesque lot of servants by offering no comment. The *nats'* rests made good towel racks, the natives were spiritually at peace, and presumably the *nats* themselves reclined nightly to their satisfaction; it was harmony without harmony, but on the surface all was well.

That same morning the headman paid me a visit —to my surprise a full-blooded Chinaman, and one of the most delightful and dramatic of my wilderness memories. With the help of three languages and two interpreters we conversed, and the substance of his formal speech was, "I have come to welcome you and to show you the valleys where the birds you seek are to be found. I trust your days spent here will bring you happiness and profit."

His bearing, his mode of delivery, matched the charm of his sentiments, and in his poise there was nothing which would not become a minister of state at any diplomatic court. So capable an actor was he, with such quick perception and sense of humor, that we soon discarded languages and interpreters, and with gestures and impromptu properties told each other of pheasants, trails and trap-building, wind, cold, danger, weapons, fatigue and distances. A few days before, three of his mules had been taken by tigers and his pantomime description of it would have held breathless the most critical audience. Some time afterward his wife—wrinkled and motherly—came to see me, bringing two chickens and a pumpkin, and presenting them with a speech, graceful and tactful as that of her husband.

The gentleness and caste of these two became all the more astonishing and inexplicable when I visited Sin-Ma-How and saw the filth and misery and squalor of the inhabitants. The huts were pitifully inadequate even as shelters, ill-thatched, inhabited equally by vermin, humanity and pigs. They were windowless and always filled with foul air, thick with smoke. These natives were in all ways of an exceedingly low order, and I found in them but one spark which redeemed them from utter degradation. This was the fervent devotion of each individual to his particular household god. No matter how poor the home, regardless of the fact that nothing more than a heap of rags formed a bed, and that one single pot sufficed for all the cooking, there was always a tiny shrine built in worship of the mysterious spirit whose privilege it was to superintend the fortunes of the family. This shrine was sacred and held in such high regard that even to have touched it would have been a desecration. In a few houses, presumably of the First Families, there was a rough bamboo scaffold on which was kept the family possessions, the pot or two, crossbows, knives, and the rough looms for weaving the sacking-like native cloth.

With these hybrid Lishao people even the normal curiosity of savages was not expressed. It was not that they were incurious, because they found the tents and every part of the equipment of such engrossing interest that they would stand for hours watching everything that took place, absorbed in every detail. But they showed in no way whatsoever the impression which these new objects made upon their minds, beyond the fact that they sometimes whispered together a few low words without gesturing or change of expression.

The conventions of dress were well established in this tribe, and even in this small village two types of women were sharply set apart, the Chinese with their pitifully malformed feet, and the Lishaos. These latter wore loose waists, high-necked with long sleeves as well as long, full skirts, with gay sashes of red and yellow. They wore also high leggins made of dark cloth, and a flowing headdress which fell like a cape over their shoulders. These costumes must have required a great amount of labor in the making, for the material was not only hand woven, but many times richly decorated with borders of shells and colored beads. Their belts were made wholly of such ivory-toned shells, linked together in some regular design, and supporting at either side two long, braided tassels which hung almost to the knees. These were sometimes weighted with copper ornaments, for copper is held in high favor by the Lishao women. They wore numberless necklaces of it—slender hoops of beaten wire strung around their necks and over their shoulders in such profusion that they were like a shining breastplate. They were suspicious and unfriendly at first, in keeping with their dull, heavy faces.

The children also give evidence of this tribal passion for ornamentation. A baby, only old enough to be carried in the cloth cradle on his mother's back, must have his beaded cap with its shells and dependent silk tassels. This is brightly colored, with high lights of copper and gives to the tiny chap an amusingly ceremonious and imperial air even while asleep. The contrast of this intricate and gaudily beautiful craftmanship when compared with the primitive filthiness and sordidness of the huts themselves was astonishing. I got a hint of the religious side of their characters from a frowsy-headed boy who sometimes went with me after pheasants. In slow and simple Burmese he talked freely of his people and his customs. He believed devoutly in the *nats,* which I gathered were nature spirits—goblins, elves, pixies—but always malevolent. The native worshipped them only that he might be let alone. At night he would empty food and drink on the ground, so that the nats might be well fed and strong to fight out their quarrels among themselves and have no time to go meddling in the affairs of those who would sleep in peace. I asked him if he had never thought that he might also be making them stronger and more capable of harming him, and this was such a new thought and evidently worried him so much that I felt as if I had meddled in something which was not my affair, and set to work successfully to kill this idea which I had thoughtlessly aroused. When the sun shone, when no thorn-sores wrought havoc with his bare feet, and when food fell abundantly from the Sahib's table, a used bowl was sufficient sacrifice at the shrine, since it symbolized the rice which was both expensive and scarce, while a few feathers implied the flesh of the fowl which the boy had eaten. So worked the native mind, in some ways not wholly unlike many who would scorn to be called heathen.

The natives of the village were harmless, but day after day, strangers came and passed, or lingered for a while, and some of these would have liked nothing better than to do us harm without being themselves caught. A gaunt, wizened man, years younger than he looked, watched us for two full days, a kindly fellow who was apparently dumb, and I am sure, quite without guile. He had an iron spear, one of the most perfectly balanced weapons I have ever had in my hand, and I tried in vain to persuade him to part with it. I offered three rupees—an unheard-of sum—and then threw in another spear larger than his, but he invariably shook his head. He waved good-by, and a few days later one of the Gurkhas returning from a hunt, brought in the poor chap's spear, and told of finding him dead and half devoured by wild beasts less than a mile away, a fact which I later verified. How he died I never knew.

On two of my trips after pheasants I had rocks rolled down upon me. The first I thought was what steamer tickets call an "act of God," such as a tidal wave, or in this case avalanche, but the second time I distinctly perceived it to be an act of two miserable Kachins, and one of the boulders bounded past less than ten feet behind my horse. A shot frightened them off and I thought no more of trouble until I sat upright on my cot one night at the tinkling of two crossed Kachin swords which I had purchased and suspended to the tent pole. Again they tinkled, and as there was no wind to explain it I took my electric flash and went outside. The Gurkha sentry had neither seen or heard anything, but at the back of the tent I picked up three poisoned arrows, spent apparently, as they had been without force enough to cut through the canvas.

The cross-bows which are used by these people are almost exactly like the weapons of medieval ages. They are drawn and set by bracing the feet against the bow and pulling back the string with both hands. The trigger is made of elephant ivory. The arrows are long, slender slivers of wood, feathered with bits of folded frond tissue, while the fire-hardened heads are barbed and the necks channelled so that they easily break off. The poison is aconite and sometimes tetanus germs. These low types of human beings of course know nothing about germs, but they do know that if the head of the arrow is smeared with dirt taken from certain places, a scratch will bring about a very unhappy death.

The sentry drew his army greatcoat well up around his face and head, and I went back to bed. For three nights this went on. I noted the direction and found a "form" of pressed grass behind a bush on the opposite hillside. One arrow had stuck in the canvas the last night, and the situation was becoming decidedly unpleasant. A scratch on the sentry's face or hand would be bad. In the daily crowd of idlers which haunted the outskirts of the camp was one surly individual of unknown tribe who carried a huge knife but was always conspicuously without a cross-bow. Toward dusk of the fourth day I made myself comfortable on the floor of my tent at the back, and watched the opposite hill with my glasses. I was rewarded just before dark and saw our camp visitor crawl into the shelter, shoving his great round hat before him with an effective-looking cross-bow and quiver of arrows in it. To my surprise an arrow struck the

The Shooter of Poisoned Arrows

From the hillside just behind, he shot at us for three nights. The evening following this photograph I shot and killed

him (see page 127)

One of My Kachin Camp-boys with a Cross-bow

This was the weapon used against us by the man in the preceding illustration

tent above me at this early hour. I did not hesitate but fired at the bush and the miserable creature rolled out and down the hillside like a ball, while alongside him, as if it were a huge, solid wheel, revolved the enormous hat. The headman of Sin-Ma-How sent up words of thanks, the Gurkhas were extremely annoyed that I had not let them handle the matter in their native way, and Aladdin's eyes were very large and his hand trembled as he served pheasant stew at dinner.

The most remarkable tragedy of this camp was that of one of my Chinaboys, Lanoo. A felon developed on one of his fingers which I lanced and bound up. The next day I saw that the bandage was off and the wound dirty. Through Lanoo's brother I advised washing and tying it up again, whereupon, without emotion, he announced that there was no use in doing this as a *nat* had entered into the wound and his brother would die in three days. The second morning the little chap lay in a state of coma and all the medicines I could give him had no effect. I tried to work on his superstitions and put him out on the sunny hillside in his blanket with a sword on top of all. There was no perspiration or other reaction to the midday heat, and the morning of the third day he was dead, and what seemed to affect the natives even more, was the fact that his favorite little white mountain pony had died during the night.

I was rather worried as to the temper of the villagers and the other Chinaboys, and I went down to the huts, leaving orders for the Gurkhas to remain behind and watch the camp. When I reached the crowd I saw that my Number One boy had disobeyed me and was following, with both hands deeply buried in his overcoat. I could not reprimand him in the presence of the natives so I ignored him. I found that the death had caused little excitement and giving the boy's brother several rupees to pay for any formalities of burial, I returned. When I called Number One and began to bawl him out for his action, he shamefacedly drew his hands out of his pockets and in each was one of his native kokris—those wicked sickle-bent knives—and he apologized, saying that any punishment I decreed was well deserved, but that his orders were to protect me. He added something which might be rendered in English as a hope that someone would start something.

I had the chance later to examine the lad's body and could find no perceptible cause of death. These people are the most stolid and at the same time the most emotional in the world and we fall very far short of fully understanding them.

Never were such wonderful days as these among the boundary mountains of the three greatest Asian countries. The sunshine seemed almost palpable in its golden glow, followed by nights so cold that I could not even remember sunshine. Nuraing Singh, my Sikh horseman, would carry into my tent the great red-hot stones upon which I had had the roaring camp-fire built, and with these under my cot I managed to keep warm for the first half of the night, after which I would shiver in spite of blankets, sweaters and raincoats for covering. In the exhilarating cold of early morning I would tear into my clothes and race around the summit of the hill to restore circulation, greatly to the edification of a few shivering natives peering from their distant huts. My trips after pheasants were heart-breaking climbs for the most part, but the results made up for everything. Often as I walked down the slope, blossom-headed parrakeets, in flocks of from two to six hundred, flew low over my head, until I was enveloped in a cloud of vibrating wings.

I found and studied silver and white eared-pheasants, Lady Amhersts, and the rarest of all monals, Sclater's impeyan. No white man had ever seen this bird alive before and there are only two or three specimens in all the museums of the world. The day of this great good fortune I woke in the early dusk, hearing only the soothing, distant roar of the streams, and now and then the footstep of the Gurkha sentry. Hardly had the jungle of the opposite slopes appeared through the cloud-drenched dawn, when the notes of a whistling thrush rose clear and sweet. A splendid, sturdy bird, making its home among the moss-hung oaks, over a mile above the sea, its song was worthy of owner and place. Its blue-black coat was still wet with dew as its throat poured forth a series of penetrating flutelike tones. They rose above the

131

roar of the torrent, and for a half hour jungle and mountain were silent, listening to this superb matin. Then, as suddenly as it began, the song ceased, and not a note was heard until dawn the following morning.

Close upon the brightening of the dawn came another sound, not of the wilderness and yet with a wildness hardly human—the pitiful wail of an insane Kachin child, which had awakened from its bitter sleep to its still more bitter daily life. Wherever it was, it strove to put its poor deformed mind upon the task of gathering a few of the myriad sticks lying everywhere in the jungle, to carry them to the hut of some native—perhaps its parents who had discarded it, or of a strange Chinese—in exchange for a mouthful of rice.

I do not know what particular death overtook these outcasts, probably starvation or leopards, but they did not survive for very long. It appeared to be the custom of this and other villages to drive out their defective children when they reached a certain age—when they were old enough to care for themselves and showed themselves unequal to the task. They drove them out into the hills, as I have said, to shift against dangers as best they could. As there was hardly food and shelter enough to go round among the able-bodied workers themselves, there was stern necessity in this and yet it appeared terribly cruel. Killing them would have been far kinder, for in the end there was always a morning when this or that one did not return to the huts to beg for the scraps of food. Sometimes two or three of them would come to my camp, always boys in their teens: The old could make no fight against such overwhelming odds. These boys were afraid of every sound and shadow, and even when talking or eating they would stand close together. Two of them would come running up the hill, holding hands, and no matter how long they stayed I never saw them release their hold upon each other. It was most pitiful in the ghastly chill of early evening to see them, still hand in hand, make their way into the forest.

One boy among them would try to talk to the Nepalese soldiers, creeping up to them when they were at work. My other servants would have nothing to do with them except at direct orders from me. The young boy's face was terrible to see, with its dark eyes looking out fearfully from under the rag of a cap. It was full of pain and questioning; his forehead was lined with wrinkles like that of an old man, and his hands and arms were covered with scars. At most he was fifteen years old. He disappeared after eight days.

The light now came quickly, and with it a multitude of birds' voices, and from the distant jungle the jubilant rollicking chorus of the jolly hoolick gibbons. Every creature here is a sun worshipper —for shade means the chill of death, and sun the bracing warmth which one can enjoy best only upon these high eaves of the world.

The sun had topped the great jagged barrier

which led straight down from the heart of the unknown north, and on our sturdy little mountain ponies we crossed a foaming stream and began a stiff zigzag climb, the trail full of deep dust and rolling stones. Now and then we came to a ledge over which the horses scrambled on knees and hocks. At the last open field we dismounted, and turned the ponies over to the Sikh. At an angle of forty-five degrees we slid, scrambled and scraped our way through the soft ground to the bottom of the ravine where the cold shade of early twilight still reigned.

Here we separated, and I made my way slowly up stream, creeping over the great rounded boulders, or wading through the rush of icy water. Every turn revealed new beauties. An enormous overhanging mass of quartz loomed up draped with swaying vines, and beyond, a little sandy bay was fretted with the tracks of pheasants, cats and deer. In the spots of sunlight among the higher branches crimson butterflies flitted about, and white-fronted redstarts dashed ahead from stone to stone.

Stopping at a favorable opening, a half-mile up stream, I began my laborious climb upward, first through a steep ascent of soft mold densely shaded by wild bananas. The undergrowth seemed scant, and as I brushed aside the first thicket of soft-leaved plants I anticipated an easy first stage. But the gray down on the myriad green stems proved scourging whips of nettle which lashed face and hands at every step. There was no

alternative, so I clambered painfully on, seizing
hold of every cold, smooth-enamelled banana
trunk as a haven from the merciless needles.

A small side ravine spread out into a broad,
fern-filled bog, and the nettles were left behind.
Then came more bananas and small evergreen
trees with little or no undergrowth. Here was the
feeding ground of the pheasants and deer. There
was hardly a square yard of mold which did not
bear the marks of the tiny hoofs of the barking
deer or the strong claws of the birds. Now and
then I picked up a feather of some silver pheasant
clinging to a bramble on the steep slope. The earth
was crumbling and again and again I fell headlong.
Once I grasped a wild banana palm, and it fell on
me—a light, air-filled stem, bearing streamers of
old, crackling leaves, and a rosette of long wavy
green ones. As I struggled, face and ears half
covered with earth, my fingers closed over something which seemed to move. I turned my head and
became suddenly sick with horror as I saw a king
cobra crawling slowly out of the fallen debris,·
fortunately making its way to the other end of the
prostrate banana stem. Its body was dull and
brown, and trailing along, crackling like the dead
palm leaves, were remnants of half shed skin. My
touch upon the sinuous body had seemingly not
disturbed it.

If it had changed its course and turned toward
me I could not have escaped from its path, half
pinned down as I was by the mass of leaves and the

stem. I watched the tapering point of the tail slowly disappear, and, weak-kneed and trembling, crept slowly off in the opposite direction.

Fortunately serpents of all kinds are rare, and this most fatal and irritable species is nocturnal, king cobras being occasionally found in the dead-falls of the natives. I had disturbed this one among the roots of the palm by my awkward fall.

I had hardly crept five yards from the place of my ugly adventure when two feathers caught my eye, and straightway I forgot my fears. They were from the plumage of no silver pheasant, but brilliant, iridescent, changeable green and purple. I was at a loss to know from what gallinaceous bird they had come. A little way farther I found another. Later, while worming my way through a barking deer's tunnel at the roots of a perfect tangle of bamboo, I heard subdued chuckles and the rustling of leaves ahead. A few feet brought me to a deeply worn but steep sambur trail, along which I made my way on hands and knees, without making a sound.

The rustling of leaves and the spray of earthen pellets falling down, came more distinctly to my ears, and at last I rested for many minutes with my face buried in a clump of blue, sweet-scented pea flowers.

Inch by inch I then edged myself upward, digging with fingers and toes into every deepened hoof-rut. A shower of earth fell upon me, and with joy I saw that a clump of soft-leaved, mint-like

Lanoo, my Chinaboy, Dying on the Hillside

His death was due apparently to superstitious fear of being possessed by evil spirits (see page 129)

Insane Kachin Boy

He came to my camp after being driven out to die among the hills

plants lay before me. I did not have to increase my numerous wounds by a slow penetration of either nettles or briers.

The revelation came sooner than I expected. Noiselessly plucking away leaves and stems one by one, to form a low tunnel, I pushed slowly and cautiously ahead. Never have I been "closer to Nature" than on this stalk. My trail was more like that of a snail or worm than of any vertebrate! Glints of light filtered through the green ahead, and I saw that a low, perpendicular bank of earth barred my way on each side. Then the forms of one or two birds appeared, and with a screen of leaves still intervening I watched what was probably the first wild Sclater's impeyan ever seen by a white man. A minute after I had reached my last position, one of the birds shook itself with all its might, sending down a shower of dirt into my eyes, while a feather or two floated off above me, down the hillside.

An inch nearer, another leaf cleared away, and I saw that there was but one bird, the appearance of the others being caused by several large mottled leaves waving about just behind the pheasant.

It was a splendid male, digging vigorously and almost continuously with its beak, working gradually around in a circle, so that I saw in turn its breast, sides and back. I watched it for five minutes when it turned, without apparent cause, but not from fright, and disappeared into the low, marshy tangle behind.

PHEASANT JUNGLES

As quick as I could lift my arm and pull up my gun from where it was dragging behind me, I fired at the still moving stems, and listened for some hint of the effect. Not a sound came forth.

I clambered up to where the bird had stood, rushed into the underbrush, and almost stepped upon the pheasant as it lay six feet from the opening. As I leaned down, trembling with excitement, two living bombs burst from the ground a few feet away—a pair of hens, or young males—and in the fraction of a second were out of sight.

On succeeding days, although I made inquiries everywhere, I could find no native who had ever seen or could give a name to this bird. The three which I blundered upon were doubtless strays from farther north, from somewhere in that mysterious land where no white man may go at present and live. Had I a yellow skin, slanting eyes, long hair and a knowledge of the twanging words which came to my ears each night from my servants' camp-fire, I might have followed these birds northward. As it is, strange people guard their haunts, neither Chinese nor Tibetans nor Kachins, but a mingling of the blood of all three, jealous of their useless land, living their bestial lives in filth and cold and squalor amid the howling winds of these heart-breaking steeps.

V

IT was in the Far East that Aladdin, Gift of God, appeared and asked for a job. In my laboratory in the Calcutta wonder house I was nailing up a box of specimens—pheasants which I had found in the North—when he walked in, bowed with gentle, melancholy dignity, and informed me that he was A. Deen, best of servants.

I was not inclined to believe this; but his personality defeated every objection. Not that he was especially prepossessing in appearance. He was small, though young and straight, with brown eyes, a chocolate skin, and an extraordinary moustache, —ragged, with a decided droop at the corners of his mouth. His personality, however, was an independent possession. It was impressive, persuasive. He had an almost theatrical appreciation of this fact. He used no other argument, offered no further evidence.

I needed a good servant. I wanted time in which to estimate him. I asked his name.

He told me, but I did not know then and I do not know now. It might have been Haladdin, yet it was not unlike Jamaldeen. "Gentlemen call me A. Deen," he added.

139

I qualified at once, and no doubt acquired caste in his eyes by saying, "A. Deen, get me a hammer and nails."

"Going, Marster," he said, and bowed so that I was enormously impressed with the seriousness of the service I had demanded.

Such was Aladdin's personality.

When he returned in a few minutes from some Chinese junk-shop, he brought with him a spike six inches long and a hammerlet which would hardly have driven home the smallest tack. I thanked him. I was well pleased. I was so well pleased that I packed them at once with my pheasants and shipped them home.

A. Deen stood by and assured me that he was indispensable to my trip, or to any trip for that matter. He was quiet about it, but he was firm. He mentioned the salary which he would consider, with assurances that he was a competent person. He insisted on this. So I gave him a pheasant and kept a discreet watch to see how he would deal with it. He made a perfect skin.

"You are engaged, Deen," I said. But I had been saddled with bad servants and I knew what it meant, so I said to myself, "A. Deen for politeness—but this is Aladdin, Gift of God."

And this proved to be far more than an etymological truth. For Aladdin was not only trustworthy, capable, loyal—a super-servant in the fullest sense: he was the living incarnation of all the best points in his people. It was through him that I saw them and learned to know something of the significant things in their lives. One cannot in a short time, or in any length of time, discover the habits, the motives, and the thousands of emotions which govern a community or a tribe of people, but one can gather unlimited information about the particular thoughts, motives, hatreds, good and evil tendencies, which govern one individual. The chip from the diamond is always a diamond no matter how small the facets or what specialized combination of colors it may chance to throw off in the sunlight.

So Aladdin was worth in many ways the price he had put on his head; a modest enough price for the West, but a somewhat pretentious one for the East.

It was from Aladdin that I learned some of those subtleties and niceties which exist between master and servant. This is a complex relation wherein each person is for a long time on probation. In civilization the difficulties are minimized, but in camp and on long mountain and jungle trips it is a test which involves strength, good temper, tact—all the elements of real diplomacy. It is a bond as intimate as friendship, with strange inequalities and reservations. It has laws, conventions, and mysterious boundaries. These are absolute.

It was Aladdin who showed me the gulf between servants and super-servants. This is a chasm as deep as the racial chasm between two tribes who live side by side, but with two codes of conduct, two sacred standards of government, of morality, of individual faith.

In civilized countries, there are good and bad servants, and this is the end of the matter. But in savage or semi-barbarous countries, there are servants and super-servants, and this is but the beginning of many things. Aladdin, himself, was the exceptional individual who was filled with a desire to separate himself from the laziness and sloth of his people, to break away from them, to see and to learn at any cost. He was moved by that inexplicable leaven which operates in any tribe or community to save one individual from the monotonous, careless existence which holds so many others chained to one faith, to one narrow, insignificant daily routine. It requires courage for him to put aside his caste, to overthrow his traditions, and humbly and modestly to make himself useful to the first white traveler who will give him something more than money for his service. It is not a brave, adventurous moment when John Perkins, butler at large in London, tenders his recommendations at the servants' door of some plutocratic mansion—he is true to his caste, his training, and his instincts. But it is an eventful hour when Aladdin, Cinghalese Malay boy, Mohammedan, presents himself with proper obeisance to a white man from over the seas and asks for a passport to the world.

So Aladdin, servant, was the superior Cinghalese

7. Siamese Fireback

8. Vieillot's Crested Fireback

of his race. With one exception I had found in Ceylon no other person of his clan whose ideals and visions and desires were not well within the circle of his caste. Ancestry had set a high wall around every Cinghalese child and woman and man who passed me in the streets. Each one walked as his father and his father's father had walked before him; talked, idled, worked, and played with the mannerisms and mentality of his great grandfather.

They were forever set apart. They were under the heel of some fixed unwritten law. Yet on their very doorstep a goodly share of the Eastern world parades up and down each day at dusk—it is a human tide that rises every time the sun sets along the sea-front of the Galle Face Hotel. The flotsam and jetsam of the East are swept along before it. Beyond, the tropical colors in the western sky are inlaid with bands of gold—and out of the heart of the glow the cool salty breeze sweeps inward from the sea. Big breakers roll in unceasingly, and patient little bullocks tug forever at big, two-wheeled carts. The drive overflows with rickshaws, carriages, and motors filled with all the peoples of the East. They touch in the crowd, but the barriers of religion and of caste move on invisible feet beside them. Mohammedan women in latticed gharries peer out discreetly at the chocolate and burnt-umber Tamil and Cinghalese girls, at Bengali, Burmese, Javanese, and Chinese folk. A stray Gurkha makes a path for himself at one side. And everywhere, in doorways and on the turf, the

Afghan money-lenders keep watch over the tide
of life as it rises and falls. No face escapes them;
their patience is endless. The costliest rickshaw
may come to them on the morrow, the dirtiest Malay vendor may return to them within the hour.
For money is the axle of the wheel wherever there
is a mint; and it is a profitable axle for the Afghans: The interest they charge is eighteen percent.

It was from such a human ferment that Aladdin
saved himself and went northward asking for a
job. It was from this that he gained the courage
to cut himself off from his people, to set aside their
laws and make himself an outcast in his own land.
For the Cinghalese do not change, therefore they
do not forget and cannot forgive. New blood has
poured in from the outside, new laws and new
faiths have claimed the driveway by the sea, but
the Cinghalese give no ground and do not stand
aside. They watch and wait, but they watch with
peaceful, untroubled faces, and the tall, circular
tortoise-shell comb that frames each head is the
comb of their ancestors and is cherished accordingly.

It is only when I look back that I realize Aladdin's rightful place among the many servants who
worked with me on my trip. He stands so far in
the foreground that I lose sight of those who are
in line behind him. This is an unconscious injus-
tice. But it was Aladdin who brought me to a
fuller understanding of the men with whom I

worked. My conscious mind was with my pheasants; I had little time to search out the individual and racial differences which separated those around me. It was Aladdin's theatrical personality which was the necessary stimulant to set in order the long chain of contrasts which were placed before me daily. I thought of the servants and super-servants who had been with me before, watched those around me, speculated upon the character and kind of those who would go with me to the countries which lay at the last of my trip. I saw them all in the new perspective which Aladdin had supplied.

Cookie, whose rightful name was Mutt, first appeared at Kuching, Borneo. It was one evening at dusk when I was sitting on the veranda of the rest-house. The tropical night was cool, and behind me in the bungalow the eccentric China-boy was pattering about softly from room to room, while I was smiling over the news that Rajah Brooke had told me in the afternoon, that a cable had come in from Singapore naïvely asking accommodations for seven hundred tourists. If I moved out, Kuching could furnish two rooms for this Caucasian horde —no more.

The air was heavy with the scent of nocturnal flowers, and the sounds that traveled with the light wind were the sounds of the East. The clang of gongs from a Chinese joss-house saluted the twilight; beyond, a noisy and colorful hubbub proclaimed a Malay wedding. A Sikh policeman called at intervals to another in the service and was answered in kind—a deep and resonant exchange of mysterious commonplaces. And far away, subdued, inevitable, minor, came from the shadows the hollow rhythm of a Dyak tom-tom.

A dark figure moved in the pathway against the darker trees. It was Cookie hastening to salaam at the bungalow steps, to offer himself for faithful service. He said that he was a good cook, and he did not lie. But although he made a free comment on his character and his personal wares, he did not offer a full explanation. It was several days after his enrollment that an important fact appeared in a casual conversation with others. It seemed that Cookie had a habit of going mad at every full moon. At certain times he had been uncommonly violent and had been put in irons. Cookie's gentle manner and epicurean sauces weighed against this tardy information; also, it was a late hour to find another cook more sane and equally competent. The lunar powers, too, favored him, for nightly no more than a slender crescent of silver showed through the dark branches. So the matter was put by with little comment. As a matter of fact, as the moon waxed full, Cookie began to ail, and on the last few days of the return trip he was hardly able to sit up.

A more faithful servant I have never had; he possessed a kindly, gentlemanly disposition which interfered in no way with his cooking. His chief physical distinction was his carriage. On the platform which served in camp for a table and chairs, he hopped about for all the world like a great awkward hornbill, while his gaudy sarong twisted and flapped and fell in folds about him like a striped flag. Mentally, he was forever taken up with two great worries. First, there was my incurable foolishness in paying good money for such useless possessions as dead pheasants, civet-cats, and snakes; second, there was that ever-present task of finding proper eggs. The Dyaks, from their love of high game, have a habit of saving, of treasuring, every egg within reach until it becomes a decidedly improper food for a more civilized taste. This troubled Cookie sorely. I believe that he mourned in secret over this tremendous tribal degeneration.

Perhaps he felt some of that helpless resignation which assails every alien when he comes unexpectedly upon the demoralizing customs that prevail in a community which is undergoing a moral and spiritual disintegration. It was just before my inland trip that I experienced this. I made a brief sojourn with the Malanos, a nondescript Malay-Dyak tribe, and saw there what corruption untimely contact with civilization may bring about. Their moral unfitness was manifest in the very atmosphere, it was proclaimed loudly in their dress. Bare legs were evidence of the savage Dyak influence; but everywhere the misunderstood canons of European fashion struggled for expression. There was something pitiful, pathetic, unbelievably naïve, in those emerald-green ties, those isolated celluloid collars, and those sleeveless cuffs which made the widest and most fantastic of bracelets: unique links in the first chain forged by a distant civilization.

With the Malanos, as with others, whatever was evil went hand in hand with all that was good. They were generous, hospitable, and my arrival was the signal for them to invent elaborate entertainment to insure my pleasure. The foremost of these events was their remarkable wrestling dance. In this, the partners, or rather opponents, sidle one about the other with the curious, lithe, serpentine glidings of the Malayan dance, until with a sudden movement they clinch, exerting all their strength in this hold for a fraction of time. The moment one dancer falls, the two of them remain absolutely posed, no matter how strained the position, how false the balance. Then gradually, to the rhythm of the wild music, they move slowly, sinuously, into the figures which are the prelude to this climax. Such a dance contains the one great dramatic element—surprise. There can be no formula for the tableau which marks the high point of emotion, each time it is a new grouping, a new portrayal of that fighting instinct which underlies every phase of existence. It gives a quality of spontaneity and of truth which a logical sequence of steps and posturings could never achieve. This indicates a keen, natural dramatic sense, but little touched by those laws and conventions which override civilized art.

Aladdin – Super-Servant

Naraing Singh

The best Sikh syce I ever had

Yat-ki and the Hybrid Yak Station

He is the second figure from the right

SERVANTS AND SUPER-SERVANTS

When the dance was done there was the cock-fight, or rather a century of cock-fights, to be reckoned with. For two hundred of these luckless creatures gladiatored bravely, while an appreciative audience held matting up to its chin to keep from being spattered with blood. Which goes to prove that hospitality is a hydra-headed creature whose spirit is sometimes finer than the faces it wears.

It was some time later—at Fort Kapit—that Cookie, but recently departed from such festivities, was fated to encounter a noteworthy rival in his particular art. This usurper was a Chinaman serving a life sentence for poisoning six people. He found no favor in Cookie's eyes; he was too good a cook. Cookie would have preferred to have the emphasis laid on his intrinsic criminality but we ate his meals and approved his service notwithstanding. It was not necessarily logical that, having poisoned six, he should harbor further ambitions.

But it was from this moment that Cookie's superior position suffered. He was submitted to all manner of petty contrasts. New servants came in and obscured him, lessened his influence. Foremost were two Malays, Matelly and Umar. Matelly was chief of one part of the crew, and he carried many minor responsibilities on his shoulders. He made quick decisions, and was unfailingly resourceful. He knew the treacherousness of the rapids and understood the recklessness of

149

the spirit who watched over the river. He was, also, an indispensable member of my interpreting quartette. I spoke English to Hodgart—super-assistant in this early part of the inland trip—who repeated the sentence in Hindustani to Matelly, who in turn notified the Dyak in his own language. After due consideration, the Dyak would, presumably, start his reply in my direction, but when it would reach home via Matelly and Hodgart it would usually be so far off key that I would give up in despair and resort to signs and sketches. This was slow work to find out the price of eggs, or the haunt of a pheasant, but the natural intuitions and active imaginations of these savages were admirable substitutes for the common language which was lacking.

Umar, who shared Matelly's prestige, was but one of the thirteen paddlers of the canoe. He differed in no essential from the twelve with whom he worked except that he wore a sarong and the other dozen Dyaks did not. But one day he became a personality of note, achieved a career in one hour. He became a money-lender, a money-lender of magnitude who diminished the glory of the great Afghans in Ceylon.

It was all a matter of good Straits dollars. When I had penetrated well into the heart of Borneo I found that money was of more use in purchasing animals and birds than the more usual mirrors, knives and scissors. Having no knowledge of the value of money other than that it was a desirable thing to possess, the Dyaks smilingly demanded enormous sums for anything they brought. To argue with them was only to arouse antagonism, so Cookie and I soon found that the best way was as follows:

A huge, naked Dyak approaches with a moon rat and a rare small bird;

"How much wanting?"

"Lima puloh ringgit."

"Flifty dollar."

"Good, here take," (giving silver coin of about eight cents value).

Result; everyone happy.

But even at this rate I found myself rapidly becoming bankrupt, and as all the specimens were of great scientific worth, I decided to send back a trustworthy man to Fort Kapit for more money. Umar was chosen. He did not want to go and pointed to the river which was swollen and running swift and high between the muddy banks.

"Big water too strong—take much days—no proper boat—how much dollar Marster wanting?" Thus spoke Umar the Malay.

Through Cookie I sent a message direct and unmistakable. "Tell Umar, No his business how much. He go quick, obey my order."

Back came the meek answer "Can lend Marster one, two hundred dollar."

At this I made large eyes of astonishment. This red-sarong-clad half-naked Malay boatman lend such a sum! The thing was incredible. His sarong and his sleeping mat were his luggage. Yet before my eyes he unfastened the small folds of his waist cloth and, with the nonchalance of Houdini producing rabbits from a hat, poured forth a flood of silver. I gave him a signed note, legal, technical and binding, for the return of a like amount on my return to Kapit, plus one additional Straits dollar. Umar the Malay affixed his mark with alacrity, and thus avoided the difficult trip down river.

I then found out that after all Straits dollars were really the least of the matter. I had scarcely noticed Umar before, he was merely one of the two Malays in my crew. But from this moment he became a personality. Now and then he made bold to essay a joke in Malay simple enough for me to understand. He now and then joined in the bargaining with strange Dyaks, where heretofore Cookie and I had wrangled alone. And the morning following his Shylockian achievement, he asked with assurance for a tiny gift of tea and sugar. But unlike so many more civilized servants, his advances ceased here, he never forgot his place in anything of importance.

One day in another month, in Darjeeling, I engaged thirty-two Tibetan coolies who were to carry the baggage and paraphernalia of the expedition over the Himalayan trails. Six of these luggage coolies were women, but women as strong and fit to cope with hardship as the men who worked shoulder to shoulder with them. I could not help but compare these people with the Veddahs of Ceylon, for these mountain coolies were boisterous, good-natured, jolly, indefatigable, frank and outspoken beyond measure. At the end of a long day's trek, when both my horse and I were thoroughly tired, I have seen several of these Tibetan women, who had kept up with me since early morning, race with one another the last hundred yards to the dâk bungalow, and make some sort of a game out of unfastening the heavy loads from their backs and heaping them up on the porch.

It may have been that the climate played a part in this. The heat of the low countries is depressing, just as the sharp cold of the hills is a stimulant. Certainly there is little in the lives of these Tibetans to make them happy. They live in eternal winter, where the snow-covered mountains look down on range upon range of white hills, and their transient homes are filthy and infested with vermin. But they are immune to suffering and privation; their excess of jubilance and joy in living spills over in the midst of the hardest labor. They laugh at everything, good or bad. They seem to have acquired some rough, instinctive philosophy which gives a bright color to the world.

One day when I was tragopan-hunting I came across one of their settlements, where eight persons and thirty-three hybrid yaks were gathered together in the semblance of a village. A single shed-like building was perched on a small, grassy platform which jutted out from the thousand-foot slope of a great Himalayan mountain, a precipitous slope dotted here and there with rhododendron-trees in full scarlet bloom. It was a sudden rift in a driving, vaporous cloud which revealed this isolated dwelling, and, when closing, shut it as quickly from view. This seemed in some way to emphasize how hopelessly these human beings were set apart from the world, to show how every outside influence must die out before it could reach them, to bring out with merciless detail the completeness of their segregation.

When I climbed down to the shed I found the people stolid, unwashed—the women hardly to be distinguished from the men. They were all of them dressed in layer upon layer of tattered, dirty cloth, and stood silent, close together, as if afraid. But after I had been with them an hour the mental and physical differences in the separate individualities became apparent. One small boy, clad in the rags of his ancestors, was the superior being among men. He stepped forward of his own accord and made friendly advances, volunteering the information that his name was Yat-ki. His small, dark face with its Mongolian eyes and typical low, broad forehead was alight with eagerness and curiosity.

This young Tibetan readily understood the business which had brought me to the mountains, and pointed out a distant gully where pheasants thrived in abundance. Also he offered his services as guide should I have need of one. He asked about my camera and when he learned that it was my ambition to point it at the yaks, drove several up to me. In all of this he conducted himself with the greatest gravity and courtesy. The other members of his clan were stupid, with that impregnable stupidity which far transcends the reputed stupidity of animals. When I was leaving and asked for the asymmetrical beaten copper jar from which I had been served with yak's milk, it was Yat-ki who engineered the bargaining which ensued, and gave the rupee which I proffered, to the owner. And when I had climbed back up the slope and turned to look down at the plateau, I saw him standing far out on the ledge, on a great boulder, waving both hands in farewell. He seemed even smaller than when he stood beside me, younger, hopeless perhaps, with the snow whirling up around him like luminous spray from the depths of the blue valley which lay so far below. He could not have been more than twelve years old, but he was centuries older than his people in sympathy, in tact, in imagination. I hope that since that day the Buddha of his Tibetan clan has dealt kindly with him.

Yat-ki brings to mind more than one other youngster of like character. I have already recorded one of these in a year and a place far distant, a coolie boy who pushed a small bunch of plantains into the freight van of the train on which I was traveling, and then sat on the steps. As the train started to move he settled himself as if for a long ride, and for a second or two closed his eyes. Then he opened them, climbed down, and swung off into the last bit of clearing. His face was sober, not a-smile at a thoughtless lark. I looked at his little back as he trudged toward his home, and wondered what desire for travel, for a glimpse of the world, was back of it all. And I wished that I could have asked him about it and taken him with me.

It seems that in every village, in every community, there is one person more gifted, more developed, than those around him. This is more apparent, perhaps, among savages or primitive tribes because their communal and personal affairs are not complete, and it is easier to know all the thoughts and motives which lie below the surface. Yat-ki, twelve years old, was a most dramatic example of this innate superiority. A few months later on this same expedition I came in contact with two other individualities, equally fine and equally set apart from the world of affairs which might have found some use for their talents.

It was when I was camped along the western boundary of Yunnan which, at the time, was in an unpleasant state of unrest and suspicion. In the little hillside village of Sin-Ma-How squalor, disease and beastly mentality reigned. And yet the headman of this Chinese-Kachin tribe and his wife stood out among their people with a conspicuousness beyond measure. He was a wrinkled Chinaman beyond middle age, a strong, dignified, lovable personality, dramatic and keen, who among his equals would have worn diplomatic robes. His wife was no less remarkable, and living in the midst of ignorance and filth, yet was gracious, tactful, and possessed that rare imagination which is the great gift, and is not to be won, courted, or in any way acquired. It was an honor to have known her, and after her grave farewell which extended to me the courtesy of her gods, I hope she thought well of me.

It was in this same region at our nightly camp-fire of great rhododendron logs that I came to know more intimately one of the most appealing of my retainers. When the embers glowed brilliantly in the utter blackness of night, I drew close, for I was camped near a high pass in the eastern Tibetan border and the icy breath from the snows siphoned down with the mist at nightfall. Twice on similar evenings I had started at the sight of a tall form looming suddenly, ghostily, from the darkness. The apparition made me reach for my weapon, for it was here that more than once poisoned arrows had rattled against my canvas, sent from the cross-bow of some Chinese renegade. But I now knew my regular evening visitor would be only Naraing Singh, the Sikh orderly, come obviously for the following day's commands, actually in the hope of a chance to talk for a few moments at the Sahib's fire.

Naraing Singh was a true Sikh and wore the five k's of his caste—the uncut hair, the short trousers, the iron bangle, the steel dagger, and the comb. And he was handsome, like most of his two million fellows, as the Greek gods were handsome, and his manners were those of a courtier. But Naraing Singh had a temperate daring which set him apart. Sustained by the thin veil of asking for orders, he stood by my camp-fire each evening, grave, respectful, attentive. I asked after the horses one by one, and ascertained that the worn girth had been mended, and I promised punishment for the syce who had driven the extra packmule over the aconite meadows, without harm, to be sure, but with a carelessness not to be condoned.

Then each evening I spoke of some subject casually, very casually, for any more direct speech would touch our difference in caste, and we should both become conscious, and the delightfully slender daring of Naraing Singh would be ended forever. It was always a subject pertaining to my own country and always of war, for the Sikh is first a warrior, and next native, orderly, syce, or what not. And his eyes would glisten, and in the flickering light I would see him sway restlessly, as a tethered elephant sways when the wind blows from scented jungle. I spoke once of the great war between the North and South, and of the battle waged at Gettysburg. After a respectful pause the question came eagerly, "At this great battle, O Sahib, at the Burg of Gettys, this Pickett Sahib, did he not charge with elephants?" And I considered gravely, and finally confessed that there were no elephants in that encounter. Ashamed to admit that our American armies were destitute of elephants, I hinted that the jungle was too thick for their use. And Naraing Singh shook his head sympathetically.

In the great Punjab and Northwest Provinces the Sikhs form a marvelous body of men. In numbers they equal the Norwegians. Their caste is high, their laws strict. They may not touch wine nor tobacco. They are not born to the title Singh, or lion, but acquire it by baptism, the water of which is called amrit, or nectar. The Sikhs form the backbone of the English native army and constabulary in India. When, as master, you win the respect and affection of a Sikh servant, you need fear neither poison nor steel in so much as it is humanly possible for him to protect you. At first it is sometimes difficult to keep the line quite distinct, to preserve the balance and distance of your relationship. For their gentle courtesy and dignity are natural and very charming, and in appearance they are the most aristocratic, handsome race of living men. As one looks deep into their clear eyes one longs for a hint of their true ancestry. It seems altogether reasonable that their forefathers were the remnants of Alexander's Grecian army, many of whom settled in the northern provinces. And the kinship of face, of morals, makes of them companions beyond all other native tribes.

When the Burma trip was done and the Ghurkas and my Sikh had returned to their homes, I was talking with Aladdin, and spoke of the wife of the headman of Sin-Ma-How.

"She was a fine woman," he said.

In the midst of all the confusion, the hurried packing, the tumult that concludes any trip, he, too, had remembered her.

I looked at him bending over a box of specimens with a hammer in one hand and nails in the other, and I was carried back to the day when he had come asking for work, which meant a passport to the world. And I thought that in spirit he was not unlike the hill-woman whom we could not forget. He, too, revealed the best in his people. I thought of all the servants and super-servants who had worked with me, and I knew that Aladdin had given me the vision to see them all in this new perspective. But I mentioned nothing of this.

Instead, I looked up from my packing and said, "A. Deen, get me a hammer and nails."

And Aladdin, Gift of God, smiled, and went quickly to do as he was told.

VI

WITH a frantic dab of my butterfly-net I scooped up a big sea-snake banded with scarlet and blue, writhing and striving to stand on his flat tail and climb out. The Chinaboy who manoeuvred the sampan against the tide screamed, "Uler laut! Uler bisa!" and even my Eurasian collector did not look happy at the approaching bagful of poisonous snake.

Like an extremely unsteady Colossus of Rhodes, I stood astride the bow, facing the racing tide, and now and then dipped up treasures which were borne toward me. This was an Alice-in-Wonderland inversion of my imagined first day in the Malay Peninsula. I had pictured mountainous jungles with their buffalo-like sladangs, with tigers and peacocks, and with gayly garbed Malays in sarong and kris. Here I was, close to shore, but marooned by red tape for a day and a night. Even the quarantine officials could find no fault with my going zoölogizing off the steamer, and so, greatly to the edification of the passengers and crew, I spent hours in scooping weird things from the swift tide.

Aside from their scientific interest, our catches were marvels of beautiful color. There were jelly-fish of opalescent silver, scalloped with sepia, alive with medusa locks—a tangle of writhing, stinging strands. To a touch of the hand these were like burning nettles, the slightest contact with any worm or crab meant death; and yet, in our glass jars, swimming in and out of the terrible tresses, were little fish, some silvery pink, others glowing with a sheen of coppery gold. Immune from paralysis and death, these small, communal creatures not only were fearless of the tentacles, but subsisted on the prey of the jelly-fish, living their whole lives as parasitic guests, unbidden, yet protected and fed by their involuntary hosts. Iridescent, feathery-footed sea-worms, pale green sea-snakes, blue translucent shrimps—all came to our net; and when the sun sank, I dabbled for phosphorescent creatures of strange forms and unknown names. With the water reflecting the tarnished silver of a lop-sided moon, I finally climbed on board, and the Chinaboy steward refused to make up my berth until the sea-snakes were safe in the alcohol tanks.

Before I turned in, I went to my favorite spot, the very point of the bow, and watched the brilliant phosphorescence. The anchor-chains of the steamer, and even my face high above the water, were brightly lighted by the baleful, greenish wave which ever rolled outward, driven by the onrush-ing tide; and overhead the green glow of the great tail of Halley's comet, sicklied by the moonlight, seemed also to partake of the phosphorescent illumination. Far up in the peak of the steamer's bow, hidden in some rusty crevice, a cricket chirped strongly, continuously, and shrilly—a tiny passenger who had sung at intervals all the way from Calcutta. He had paid no fare, and to-night he might, if he chose, defy the quarantine which kept me so impatiently immured. He would spread his wings and fly ashore to this strange region so many hundreds of miles south of the low marshes of the Hoogly.

My second day in Malaysia was almost spoiled by an attempt to eat a durian. Eating a durian, or, as in my case, essaying to do so, is an experience not soon lost to memory. Its achievements must be productive of a noticeable growth of ego. I often think how I should enjoy being able casually to boast, "I have eaten durians in the East," or, "This tastes as good as a durian." The durian has a powerful personality. It is large and green, not unlike a breadfruit, and it is covered with unpleasant spikes. But these, I am told, are no deterrent to the man or beast who has once acquired the durian habit—who, by complete suppression or mortification of the organs of smell, has succeeded in swallowing even a section of the fruit. It grows on tall trees, and natives will sit for days waiting for a ripening durian to drop. White children, once inoculated, prefer it to all other fruit; tigers will approach close to Malay villages, risking their

lives to vary their carnivorous diet with a mouthful of durian.

If simplicity in diction indicates strength, I will
state tersely that the durian has an odor. In de-
ference to passengers who are not durianivorous,
Lascars are forbidden to bring the fruit on any
tourist steamer. Yet if a stoker in the deepest
coal-bunker has broken the rule and smuggled one
on board, his brother on the lookout in the crow's
nest will soon know and become envious. With
rotten eggs as a basis, if one adds sour milk and
lusty Limburger cheese ad lib., an extremely unpleasant mixture may be produced. It quite fails,
however, as an adequate simile to durian. The
odor and taste of durian are unique, unparalleled,
and they did not pass from my mind during my
second Malaysian day. I am at a loss to explain
why durian is not the favorite food of vultures and
the exclusive preoccupation in life of burying
beetles.

As thoroughly as my first day in Malaysia had
been circumscribed by quarantine and salt-water,
so was my second hectored by kindness. Within
tantalizing sight of distant jungles, conscious of
the calls of strange birds and the scent of wild
blossoms, I had perforce to make my manners to
courteous officials who, with their wives, left nothing of entertainment undone. Over beautiful
roads I was swiftly motored to a most interesting
laboratory for the study of tropical disease. Here
were yardfuls of most amusing-looking fowls, all

apparently in the last stage of intoxication. They staggered about, stepping on their own toes, and looking as mortified as it is possible for hens to look. As a matter of fact, they were temporarily paralyzed by a diet of polished rice. A change to the unhusked rice, rich in phosphorus, would at once restore health. The condition corresponded in all particulars to beri-beri, the disease so common among the rice-eating Malays.

From the laboratory I sped through the dust to a wonderful botanical garden, one which had been accorded heedful care for many years, with great trees and palms, luxuriant tropical shrubs, and giant Malayan orchids with flower-stalks seven feet in length. Here magpie-robins and drongos, ground doves and bulbuls nested or sang, and here all seemed peaceful. And yet the very sense of undisturbed rest, of balance and permanence, was fraught with a deep sense of unreality. Within a month this entire valley was to be dammed and filled to the brim with reservoir water, and all these lakes and drives, the arbors and elaborate flower-beds, the palms with their birds' nests, and the myriads of other contented homes, would be buried many yards deep in cool, fresh water. The impending doom of all plants and all sedentary animal life was intensely oppressive. It was far more ominous than the presage of a disastrous storm, infinitely more portentous than the approach of a northern winter. To the imagination it was as appalling as the onrush of an over-whelming forest fire.

The only observation which remains in my memory was strange enough to be significant of the abnormal fate of these beautiful gardens. I saw a young duckling killed and partly pulled under, and when I looked carefully into the troubled waters I was astonished to see that the bird had been slain by an insect, one of those great water-bugs which in the States are commonly known as electric-light or kissing bugs. The powerful insect had submarined up and driven its beak deep into the breast of the duckling, which had died after a few futile struggles.

From this valley of the shadow I was hurried on to the usual country club, clock-golf and tea, and then the inevitable formal dinner. Not until the exhausting day was at last at an end did I realize the splendid spirit of hospitality which prompted it, and I knew that I should duplicate the experience whenever any of these rare-souled English folk found their way to New York, around on the opposite side of the planet.

Late in the evening I walked through the native quarter of the town of Kwala Lumpur. Then for the first time I began to appreciate how completely the Chinese are elbowing the Malays to the wall. The latter are excellent syces and grooms, but in all other capacities one thinks only of Mongolians.

Even at this late hour one tiny photographer's

shop was open, with the proprietor, a short but clean-limbed young Chinaboy, squatted just within. His eyes were narrowest of slits, his pipe with its microscopic bowl was held lightly between his teeth. He might have been fast asleep. But at the first indication of my hesitancy, of my prospective interest, Chinaboy rose swiftly, his pipe vanished, and his eyes opened to ovals. Smilingly I was wished "Goodleevling."

In days to come Chinaboy did work for me and did it well, and I was the richer for knowing him, for watching his quiet assurance, his unassuming dignity. But best of all was his story, which was narrated with insight and imagination by the wife of a government official. It is a tale which is duplicated daily, perhaps hourly, wherever Malay and Chinese come into contact,—a tale of the quiet usurpation, by thrift and steadiness of purpose, of almost every field of endeavor by these patient Mongolians.

Not many months before, in this very street, Anggun Ana, photographer, kept a tiny shop— ugly, untidy, built of rough boards as are most Malay shops, and not particularly cleanly within. In every way it resembled its owner, except that Anggun Ana was not ugly. A lazy man is always good-natured, and no good-natured person is really ugly.

On his counter lay an untouched order. It was a hard job of films of assorted sizes, and he did not like it. For two hours Anggun Ana sat in the doorway wondering whether to begin work on them the next morning or the morning after.

"Am velly good Chinaboy," said a liquid voice in his ear, rousing him from a doze. "Can dust, sleep floors, eat velly little." Chinaboy, neatly clad in a faded smock and a braided queue, stood before Anggun Ana and made a low bow, which tickled the pride of the Malay. "Am velly good boy," insisted the small Mongolian, explaining that he would work for his rice and a place to sleep.

Anggun Ana considered the applicant with patronizing outward gravity and inward jubilation. After the prolonged haggling which the East demands before the consummation of the smallest bargain, he engaged him at his own terms,—one bowl of rice a day,—conveying the impression that he was thereby doing Chinaboy an immeasurable favor. The latter seemed to have no word with which to express his gratitude. Slowly and earnestly, three times, with many bows, he said "Muchee 'blige!"

Chinaboy, apprentice, attended punctiliously to business for Anggun Ana, photographer. He swept, dusted, cooked, and studied the inner mysteries of photography, while his master dozed in the shade. At night he slept under the counter, with his ever more faded blue smock, which he had washed before nightfall, spread out on the line to dry. Chinaboy omitted no detail of duty, wasted no time in play, won the approval of his master, and held himself in constant readiness for the opportunity which an optimistic mind always knows is just ahead.

One day, six months later, an Englishman brought in some films—a large order which must be done at once. Anggun Ana had gone to the corner to buy some sweet cakes. The Englishman suggested that Chinaboy go search for his master immediately. But the latter shrugged his shoulders, gathered the films in his apron and said, "Can do," with such modesty and assurance that the Englishman agreed to the bargain.

The films and prints were delivered at the hotel two hours before the appointed time, with no mistakes and the work well done. A few more tourists dropped into Anggun Ana's shop in the next two months. Each time the proprietor was out and Chinaboy did the work—and kept the money.

Then one night a new little bandbox of a shop budded off from the godown across the street. Chinaboy had graduated from his apprenticeship. He had moved up to the grade of proprietor, as his brightly painted and incorrectly spelled sign indicated. His shop was clean, always clean, and tidy, and orders were executed promptly even when Chinaboy had to work all night to finish them. Into a black lacquer box trickled a thin, yet surely swelling stream of money. On the day the box was filled, Chinaboy walked across the street and bought out Anggun Ana at his own price, just as months before he had bargained to work at his own price.

Anggun Ana is now attached to a planter's menage and sleeps near the horses. Chinaboy has moved down to the corner opposite the hotel and employs three assistants, none of them Malays.

Thus the steady, quiet, unyielding conquest of Malaysia is being carried forward by Chinaboys —first immigrants, later apprentices, and at last proprietors. They come from an over-crowded, impoverished land which only reluctantly yields its increase. They are trained to industry, tenacity, and thrift. Before their attack the good-natured, slow-moving, indolent Malay goes down to quiet, certain defeat. In my short evening's walk I had abundant opportunity to observe the lesser, subtle workings which in due time will effect racial distribution in all the Far East. People were dominant in my mind; the jungle was for the morrow.

Three hours of intensive effort the next morning set various people and official departments in motion, perfecting arrangements for the trip into the interior. When I had given it sufficient impetus, I turned the matter over to competent hands, Aladdin's and others, and made my way as speedily as I could to the nearest jungle. I could hope only for a short plunge today, and on the advice of a bronzed planter, whose love of the wilderness shone in his eyes when I told of my coming trip, I motored out to a bukit, or mountain, in which were some interesting limestone caves.

My day with these caves was unforgettable.

Double Entrance to the Batu Caves, Pahang

Heart of the Malay Jungle

Home of the ocellated and bronze-tailed pheasants

FROM SEA TO MOUNTAIN-TOP

Gulliver and Alice and Seumas might have accompanied me and would not have been bored, so strange were the great caverns. Even the approach held something of mystery, for while they were etched into the base of a high precipitous mountain, this was invisible until one stood suddenly before it. After passing along roads beaded with thatched coolie huts and little Chinese shops, the purring motor turned into a lane-like path and I drove past all the rubber trees in the world— thousands and thousands of them. Like the rows of pulque plants on the Mexican uplands, the trunks of the rubber trees seemed to revolve as I passed, like the spokes of some gigantic horizontal wheel. Then we stopped suddenly, and looking up I saw a great cliff looming high overhead. It was clothed in green, except where it was out at elbow with patches of raw, white limestone. Before I left the car, a strong scent—unpleasant, exciting, and entirely strange—was wafted down on some current of air from the cave.

A stiff climb of a hundred yards brought me to the mouth of the dark cave—a great, gaping, black hole, the edges draped with graceful vines. I entered and, after going a hundred feet, looked back and saw an exquisite bit of the tropical landscape: palms, distant blue mountains, and white clouds framed in the jet-black, jagged aperture.

The great height was overwhelming; the graceful dome-like summit of the cavern stretched up and up into the very vitals of the mountain. Then

I plunged into darkness and lighted my electric searchlight, which seemed at first the merest bit of light ray. On and on I went, and at last, far in the distance, perceived a faint glimmer from high overhead. A rustling sound at my feet drew my light downward, and there were untold thousands of great brown cockroaches, all striving to bury themselves out of sight in the soft, sawdust-like flooring, the century-old guano of the bats. I had to go with great care, for huge jagged rocks and deformed stalagmites obstructed the path in every direction.

I reached the rift in the lofty roof, and the glare blinded me for the moment, although it was tempered with a tracery veil of green. I had already begun to adapt myself to the everlasting darkness. At my feet the light fell softened, diluted with a subterranean twilight. In the centre of this part of the cave, directly under the cleft in the roof, was a curious, gigantic stalagmite, still forming from the constant dripping two hundred feet overhead —a stalagmite of great size and extreme irregularity. The first casual glance showed it vividly to the eye as two weird, unnamable beasts struggling with each other. No feature or limb was distinct, and yet the suggestiveness of the whole was irresistible. Virile with the strength of a Rodin, the lime-saturated water had splashed it into visibility, depositing the swell of muscles and the tracery of veins through all the passing years, to the musical tapping of the falling drops. And in all the great extent of the passage of the cavern, the statue had been brought into being in the only spot where it would be visible by the light of the outer world.

For a long time I sat here, finding the odor of the bats less pungent than elsewhere, and here I watched the ghostly creatures dash past. From the inky darkness of some hidden fissure they dropped almost to my face; then, with a whip of their leathery wings, they turned and vanished in the dark cavern ahead. The noise their wings made was incredibly loud; sometimes a purring, as fifty small ones whirred past together, then a sharp singing, and finally an astonishing whistling twang as a single giant bat twisted and flickered on his frightened way.

Another sound was the musical, hollow dripping of slowly falling drops on some thin resonant bit of stone, a metronome marking the passing of inky black hours and years and centuries; for in this cavern there are no days. Every noise I made, whether of voice or footfall, was taken up and magnified and passed upward from ledge to ledge, until it reached the roof and returned again to me. It was changed, however,—wholly altered; for it seemed that no sound of healthy creature could remain pure in this durable darkness, the sepulchre of unburied bats, the underworld of hateful, bleached things, of sunless, hopeless blackness. The obscurity seemed, by reason of its uninterrupted ages of persistence, to have condensed, the ebony air to have liquefied. There was no twilight of imagination, inspired by knowledge of coming day. Only quiet, eternal night.

From the black gulf ahead came, now and then, low distant mumblings, mingled with the shrill squeaks of the bats, and into this vocal void I now plunged, with the searchlight playing at my feet to avoid tripping and falling. I found that I had entered a veritable Dante's Inferno, and pictured to myself some still more dreadful round as presently to open out ahead. The sighing, gibbering, squeaking spirits or devils were there in multitudes, brushing my face or fighting among themselves as they clung to the slippery fissures high, high overhead. More than once my light led me down a small, blind side lane, into which I stumbled as far as possible. At the end of one such corridor was a roundish hole leading irregularly downward, far beyond the rays of my light. Another contracted very slowly, until the damp walls touched my head and sides and I drew nervously back, glad to escape from the sense of suffocation —as if the walls were actually closing about me, inevitably, irrevocably.

Every stone I overturned revealed numbers of tall, slender spirals—the homes of dark-loving snails; and ever the roaches in their myriads hurried away from my light. Then I came upon tragedy—fitly staged in this black hell. A commotion on the black mould directed me to where a poor bat had recently fallen, having by some accident broken his shoulder, and lay, like fallen Lucifer, gnashing his teeth and helplessly turning from side to side. More than this, two horrible gnomes fled at my approach—a long, sinuous serpent, white from its generations of life within the cave, and a huge centipede, pale, translucent green, sinister as death itself. I shuddered as I beheld this ghastly tableau,—serpent and centipede both emblematic of poisonous death, preparing to feast upon a yet living bat, devil-winged and devil-faced.

The predatory ones escaped me, though I wanted the snake. I put the bat out of his misery, his evil squeaking rage at fate remaining undiminished to the very last breath. On his nose were the great leaves of skin which aided him in dodging the obstacles in his path of darkness—organs which had failed him for a fatal moment.

Farther on I turned sharp corners and wound my path around strange angles, disturbing unending hosts of bats and finding many recently dead, together with innumerable skeletons half buried in the guano. Now and then a centipede fled from my tiny pencil of light, and once I broke open a nest of stinging ants, blind but ferocious, which attacked me and made me flee for several yards headlong, heedless of bruising, jagged obstacles.

Then my feet sank suddenly in ooze and water, and, flashing the light ahead, I saw it reflected from the ripples of an underground river flowing with no more than a murmur out of one yawning hole into the opposite wall of the cavern, mysterious as the Styx. Beyond this I might not pass. The current was swift and it was far over my depth. I had no wish to be swept deep into the bowels of these mighty Malay mountains, although the Nibelungs might well have chosen such a place for their labors.

From Kwala Lumpur to Kwala Kubu is only a few miles by an energetic little railway, which lurches and pitches sideways, but in spite of this never ceases to advance. The time passed quickly, as I chugged and jerked over the rails the next day, for I had two antithetical diversions. I could look out of the window and instantly yield to the hypnotic spell of the revolving wheel of the rubber trees, rendered more pastel and potent by the intervening mist of driving rain. Or, consulting my bethumbed handbook of Malay, I could mumble, *Buleh kasi habis kasut itu?* One sentence I omitted, making no effort to learn: *Pergi ka pasar beli buash durian satu biji,* which, being translated is, Go to the market and buy me a durian!

When I alighted at the forlorn, drenched little station I called out to Aladdin, *Panggil kuli tiga orang!*

He smiled, and three coolies were summoned at once, and over me crept the glow which such pseudo-linguistic ability ever brings to one who is altogether without natural talent in this direction.

In the dâk-bungalow at Kwala Kubu, the Chinaboy chowkidar, queue in pocket, shod in shoes of silent felt, served my breakfast. I was at last on the threshold of a strange expedition in a land to which no letter ever came correctly addressed, so unknown was it to the outside world. At this moment the strangest thing in sight was my breakfast. It consisted chiefly of tins of tiny Mongolian finches,—hummingbirds in size, squabs in taste,—canned a dozen to a tin.

As I devoured the pitiful little birds, bones and all, I looked up at the great Malay mountain-range, the backbone of the finger peninsula which stretches southward from Siam to within sight of the bund of Singapore itself. Mountains, so the Malays say, are the walls of the world, shutting out great winds and beasts of prey. And they believe that a strange race—the Yajuj—are forever striving to bore through, and when they succeed, then will come the end of all things. The great limestone caves scattered throughout the mountains are places where the Yajuj have attempted and failed. There is nothing impossible or unbelievable in all this, when one comes to know Malay mountains in all their weirdness.

At this moment, across the high range, there wandered slowly through the jungle pheasants, giant ocellated argus—pheasants never yet seen alive by a white man. I knew that somewhere in that great unexplored tumble of mountains they lived, and it was to find them and their kindred that I had come half round the world. But now I had no time to think of them or of possible means of discovering them, for Aladdin, super-servant, rushed up as fast as his newly donned Malay sarong skirt would permit, and breathlessly announced, "Sahib, lorry ready." So I had to don my pith topee and regretfully leave three squablets swimming in their butter sauce; for the motor lorry was wheezing and spitting, and His Majesty's mail waits for no one.

Thus I made my ascent to the summit of the great mountain range, amid a continuous whirl of choking dust which quite obliterated the scenery. I might have imagined myself caught up in a cloud, as worthy biblical characters were wont to be, only I am sure they were spared the odor of burning oil and rubber, and their ears were not assailed with a syncopated obstruction in the brake mechanism which, before the end of the trip, vied with the efforts and effect of any brain-fever bird.

When we emerged from our cloud and excavated our eyes we found a wonderland, a little rose-covered dâk cottage with an immaculately saronged Cinghalese in attendance, and tiffin of curry and tea. This was Semangko Pass—the Darjeeling and the Simla of the Malay Peninsula.

Semangko Pass struck deep into memory as the most beautiful of the tropical mountains of the East where I strove to match my senses against those of the jungle pheasants. The dâk was perched on a little flat saddle at the very crest of the ridge, scarcely less than three thousand feet above the blue waters of the Indian Ocean. On all sides the sharp-toothed mountains rose still higher, steep but jungle-clad, cutting the sky into all sorts of irregular bits of glory.

The days were wonderful, and the alternations of sun and wind were as exciting as the discovery of the strange Malayan beasts and birds. The sun rose softly—no breeze moved cloud or leaf, and even the light came at first moderately, indirectly, reflected from the higher peaks, or heliographed from the mirror of a half-hidden, distant water-fall. In early afternoon—one never knew just when—the faintest of breezes sifted down and blurred the lacery of tree-fern shadows. The wind was cool and soon strengthened, and by night the air was surging violently through the gap, si-phoned from the cold summits down to the hot, humid valleys.

Day after day one reawakened to the sense of tropical surroundings from a conviction of a north-ern autumn, with the wind full of swirling leaves and the fronds soughing with the same sad cadence as the needles of scented pines of the northland.

The first night I listened to this strange sound of wind in the eaves of the bungalow, and the moans of the engineer's fever-stricken little baby, brought here for relief from the hot coast. And then I slept, and was awakened by the distant, faint chorus of wa-was, the long-handed gibbons, a sound as thrilling, as full of age-hidden memory meaning as the morning chant of the red howlers in the South American jungles.

The liana-draped trunks and the majestic jungle trees were the finest in all the East, second only to those of Amazonia, but the tree-ferns were beyond words—tall, graceful, with great unfolding fronds half-clenched, swathed in wool of richest foxy-red. Here, in this maze of mountain jungle, through its autumnal days and its wild, tropic nights, lived two splendid races of birds. One was the bronze-tailed peacock pheasant, the other the giant ocellated argus. Each was a challenge to my utmost effort. Neither had been seen by a white man; of neither had we any facts of home or courtship, food or foe.

So in khaki and moccasins, with gun and glasses and compass, I stepped into the filmy shadows of fern-fronds drooping high above my head, and essayed to awaken my senses from the dulling erosion with which hotels and formal dinners, railways and motors had overlaid them. Never have I encountered more worthy antagonists, and I was proud in the end to be able to record one victory and one drawn battle. I found the peacock pheasants. The ocellated argus I heard and trapped, but the sight of a living bird awaits a better woodsman than I.

The Selangor side of the pass seemed to be pheasantless, so I worked chiefly to the east, in Pahang itself. I climbed the steep, upsloping jungle to an elevation of nearly forty-five hundred feet, creeping laboriously through bamboo tangles or holding on to long liana guy ropes, along precipitous, pathless banks. Sometimes the going was so heartbreakingly rough that I progressed only a mile in a half-day's tramp.

It was on one of these trips that I scored victory and saw the first bronze-tails. Late one afternoon I reached a steep land-slip which, a few months before, had carried away a wide swath of jungle, leaving the disintegrated rock exposed or decorated with the new-sprouted plumes of yellow green bamboo. I had had a long, tiresome tramp, and was two miles from camp, across a deep, dark valley. At the edge of an open glade, sheltered by dense bamboos and close to the crest of a sharp ridge, I waited for an hour or longer—a lucky hour as it proved. After removing the usual unpleasant collection of leeches, I sat quietly and watched the jungle life about me. A single tall tree leaned far out over the great earthen scar, its roots half exposed, soon to loosen and end its century of growth in an ignominious slide to the tangle far below.

From the topmost branches several bronzed drongos were flycatching and uttering their loud chattering song. A sudden *whoof! whoof!* of wings sounded close overhead and four heavy-pinioned hornbills alighted awkwardly, each striking its hollow anvil in turn, the air fairly ringing with the deep metallic sound. Then one of the birds discovered me, and the four swept off again with outstretched necks and a roar of wings.

Ten minutes later a tupaia, or tree-shrew, ran out along a dead bamboo stem and began to pull off the sheaths, poking his sharp nose under them, presumably after insects. A second appeared and thereupon ensued a fight of the fiercest character. At first it was a pursuit, the two flying along bamboos, up tree-trunks, and even leaping three feet or more through the air. They closed at last on a branch and the fur flew from the mass of twisting limbs and bodies. Then over they went, separated in mid-air, and each stretched out his four legs to the fullest extent. Close to me they dropped, both landing on the great fronds of a tree-fern. They caught hold, rested panting a moment, and then vanished.

Hardly had they gone when a distant movement caught my eye and I looked intently along the ridge. There, in full view, were three bronze-tailed pheasants, apparently looking directly at me, although a screen of bamboo leaves intervened. I soon saw that the sudden fall of the tupaias was what had attracted their attention. As I watched, two others appeared. They remained in sight about four minutes. One of the old birds never stirred from the spot on which I first caught sight of him, —head raised, alertly turning now this way, now that. The others moved about, stepping daintily and high. Two scratched for a while in the rain-washed gravel, one of them soon turning its attention to a clump of yellow flowers, picking the blossoms and swallowing them eagerly.

One of the adult birds stepped into a spot of full sunlight, the last which penetrated the foliage

from the setting sun, and for a moment fluffed out
every feather. The wings were lowered, the tail
spread, and thus for a full minute did the splendid
bird do homage to the last rays of the sun. The
gray head and breast were alive with the tiny white
spots which showed as living sparks in the sunlight.
Each feather of the rich rufous upper plumage
seemed consciously aglow through its individual
eye, as if it could see itself reflected in the gorgeous mirrors of the tail. These long tapering
feathers were spread apart and their surfaces
changed from green to violet, then to purple and
back to emerald again as the angle shifted. I fairly
held my breath for fear of putting an end to the
rare display. At last the sun's ray died away, and
simultaneously the bird's tail closed and hid the
iridescent glory of the feathers. With low clucks
the little covey walked slowly into a fern tangle.
I hastened to the crest of the ridge, but neither saw
nor heard anything more of the birds, though I
could look far down into the damp, dark depths of
the ravine, through a maze of bamboo columns and
feathery fronds.

From a great distance came the bass and treble
of the wa-was, rising in wild, rollicking cadence.
A fraying end of cloud-mist drifted past, warning
me that a storm was brewing; and the shrill, metallic ring of the six o'clock bees marked the swift
approach of dusk. I knew that the wild creatures
of the night were walking all about me, from the
tiny civets which would soon start out in search of

mice and insects, to the black leopard, whose roar I had heard the night before and whose fresh track I would pass on the way to camp. Once I was startled by a sudden rush and squeak, but it was only a spiny-haired rat fleeing from some unknown danger. The darkness settled down as I reached my hammock, emphasizing the many spicy jungle odors and ushering a wind which rattled the bamboos and shook every loosened leaf to the ground.

It is difficult to write of the great ocellated argus pheasant because of the indescribable marvel of itself and its life. Its myriad-eyed wing feathers, its complex courtship display, its secret dancing-ground in the heart of the jungle—all set it apart as a bird superlative and distinguished. In its great specialization of pattern and habit it has achieved a position perhaps furthest from its lizard-bird ancestry. Wary as it was, and much rarer than the giant gray argus, I made out to patch together a fairly satisfactory life-history from bits gleaned here and there—a deserted nest, a dancing-ground, a freshly trapped bird. Thrice my relations with it verged upon intimacy, when I just missed seeing it. And the very failure, the suspense never wholly to be lifted, impressed the details more vividly on my mind.

Once I watched—as always, alone—by a clearing which I supposed to belong to a gray argus; but after an hour, an ocellated argus pheasant approached, coming nearly within sight and then circling warily about. As I sat quietly amid the swaying stems of bamboos and the trembling fronds of tree-ferns, babblers in families, and small birds in loose flocks of several species occasionally passed, on their twittering, fly-catching paths of life. It was late afternoon and the creatures of the jungle were making the most of the last hours of daylight. Gaudily colored squirrels leaped overhead, and now and then a tree-shrew pushed his sharp muzzle around a neighboring trunk and stared at me, but unaccountably did not give the alarm. Close to me a bee-eater—lilac-fronted, flame-breasted—swooped after the dancing gnats. Long-tailed drongos were courting a small, unornamental female—three of them swooping about her at one time. As they flew and dipped and volplaned, the two round feather-racket tail-tips swept after them, apparently wholly unconnected by any physical bond. Two cock broadbills fought continually, with constant enthusiasm and equal discretion. In the rare intervals between their long-continued bouts, both repaired to the upper air, high above the forest, for refreshment, and there soared about, for all the world like diminutive vultures, now and then dashing sideways after an insect. Small green parrakeets quartered the pheasant's clearing again and again, and a pair of giant, sombre-hued woodpeckers, bigger than ivorybills, hammered vigorously, sending down chips upon the cleared arena.

All these voices and sounds seemed to show that

there was no danger near; the usual life of the jungle was undisturbed; but the pheasant knew better. I had neglected some little precaution, and some stray strand of suspicious evidence had warned the bird that all was scarcely well. The woodpeckers might hammer and the drongos scream, but he was conscious of a something which drew a dead-line about his arena. He called, but half-heartedly, and after a reconnaissance he returned to some unknown covert. I could not let him know that I had no gun and that a half-hour's watch of his unconscious jungle life was all for which I hoped.

Another time only a transient physical disability prevented me from seeing one of these birds. An ocellated pheasant had been calling at dusk, and on my way back to camp I turned aside and followed a narrow game-trail to a stream. A loud rustle made me crouch low, but the animal, whatever it was, made its way off. I waited for five minutes and then the call of the great bird rang out directly behind me. So loud was it, I thought at first it came from overhead. Then a second time, and my ears rightly oriented it as a few yards behind. The light was failing. In a few minutes it would be dark, and I could hear the bird moving. I was hidden by a barrier of scrub. I attempted to leap to my feet and turn as I rose; but instead I merely fell awkwardly backward. Both of my feet were paralyzed, asleep, and would not support me. A second effort succeeded and I saw the swaying stems close together behind the fleeing bird, but had never a glimpse of even a tail-feather.

My third experience was the most thrilling of all. Along the central Malayan range of mountains, on the Pahang side, rise innumerable little streams, mere rills at first, which soon gain in volume, rill added to rill, until a good-sized brook bubbles over the rocks and slides smoothly over fallen bamboo stems. Wading and splashing along these streams-beds is by far the most convenient means of exploring this region. Often the sides of the ravines are so precipitous that it is impossible to pass across or along them.

For two nights I had slung my hammock from the giant grasses beside one of these tiny Pahang tributaries and had listened to a new sound. At frequent intervals, for a half-hour at a time, the loud call would ring out. It was almost the call of the great gray argus, but there was a strange intonation which attracted my attention at once. I realized at last that it was the evening call of the Malayan ocellated argus pheasant. While I never heard the calls of both species in the same evening, yet the difference was very marked. There was a muffled resonance about the cry of the ocellated bird which the cry of the other lacked; it sounded fully as loud, but was without that penetrating quality which carried the tones of the argus through fern and bamboo, over ravines and jungle slopes, to such great distances. It was more harmonious, less harsh.

PHEASANT JUNGLES

Disregarding the rumors of tigers and black leopards, I crept through the jungle in the dead of night, the damp mist rising thickly from the reeking ground about me, and the white trunks of the jungle trees looming up like ghosts. I made my course by compass and broken lianas and laid it by the occasional wild scream of the bird. Finally I seemed to be approaching. Nearer and nearer sounded the call, appearing almost as if the bird were walking toward me. Then my electric search-light showed an impenetrable tangle of rotan and thorn-palms—a maze of myriad recurved hooks. Even in bright daylight one might not pass through this without laboriously cutting a trail, foot by foot.

So here I waited, crouched at the foot of a clump of lofty bamboos, my light shut off, and realizing as never before, the mystery of a tropical jungle at night. A quarter of a mile away, the magnificent bird was calling at intervals, from just some such place as I was in. When my eyes recovered from the glare of the light, I found that the jungle was far from dark. The night was moonless and not a glimmer of star came through the thick foliage overhead. But a thousand shapes of twig and leaf shone dimly with the steady, dull, blue-green phosphorus glow of fox-fire.

Once a firefly passed through the bamboos—a mere shooting star amid all these terrestrial constellations. The mould beneath my feet might change to peat, or, in future ages, to coal, but even then the alchemy of fire would be needed to awaken the imprisoned light. Here, from plants still erect, which were blossoming but a short month ago, a thousand gleams shone forth, defying the blackness of night.

Some small animal passed to windward of me, sniffed, and fled at full speed. The wings of a bat or other flying creature whistled near, while ever the resonant call of the ocellated bird rang out, mocking my helplessness. The firefly could make its way through tangle and thorns to the very spot where the bird stood: any small four-footed creature of the night could creep noiselessly over dried bamboo sheaths until his little eyes marked the swelling throat of the calling pheasant: But here was I, with a powerful electric light, with the most penetrating of night-glasses, with knowledge of savage wood-lore, and with human reasoning power; and yet with feet shod with noise, with clothing to catch on every thorn—a hollow mockery of a lord of creation!

Again the bird called, and I interpreted its message: The law of compensation! I was helpless to reach it, I was degenerate indeed in the activities of the primitive jungle-folk, but I thrilled at the mysteries of the nocturnal life. My pulse leaped at the wild call—not from a carnivore's desire for food, or from the startled terror of the lesser wilderness people, but because of the human-born thirst for knowledge, from the delights of the imagination which are for man alone.

VII

I SQUATTED cooliewise on a fallen tree-trunk, poised gingerly on my toes, for the leaves about me were all aquiver with hungry leeches. Behind me was the rose-colored dâk bungalow of Semangko Pass, on the crest of the Malay mountain range. In the compound the mail-lorry smoked and snorted and resented every attention which the Chinaboy mechanic paid to the reluctant engine. Before me, and far beyond intervening valleys, stretched the bamboos and tree-ferns of the Pahang hinterland, whither I was bound.

At this very moment, across the ranges, far to the eastward of my fallen tree, a sultan and his court and nobility, armed with kris and knife, and clad in silks and satins of rose and blue and emerald, were making their way slowly to the central square of their town, eager to begin the day of their top spinning. Nearer to my dâk, close under the lofty jungled heights, deep within a blind, hanging valley, six white men weltered in the stifling heat and planned the impossible—the combatting of virulent cholera among superstitious Malays. And nearer still were wild men of the mountains,—Sakais, almost monkey-like in their

190

Water Buffalos

The greatest danger of the white explorer in the East

The Trail to Kuala Lipis over the Backbone of the Malay Mountains

life, and wandering lepers with dissolving surfaces which once were faces.

And in the same country with all these people whose lives were respectively so incongruous, so altruistic, and so pitifully hopeless, threading the bamboos and the tree-ferns, were wonderful pheasants, indescribable argus, and green peacocks in flocks. These I sought, and of these alone I thought as the hectic horn of the mail-motor gave forth a cracked, blatant blast. I rose, flicked off a few threadlike leeches hastening over my puttees, and made my way back to the dâk compound, the little level acre balanced on the shoulders of the mountain pass, filled with roses and the odor of burning oil and ill-mixed gasoline. I crawled into the uncomfortable motor lorry and began the next stage of my journey.

Far behind, as we left the higher altitudes, the last tree-ferns and bamboos disappeared, and here we found dense jungle tangles, warped and woofed with thorny rotans and climbing canes, while every open spot was self-sown with coarse elephant grass. Kuala Lipis is very near to one's visualization of Hades, so it was appropriate that the mail-lorry should always arrive in weltering heat, with blistered rubber tires and boiling engine.

From the small shadow of the dâk veranda I looked through the glaring heat across to a few scattered hospital buildings. A dozen yards down the white dusty road was the single store, and behind was the inevitable clubhouse. Beyond these,

191

in all directions, rose the irregular heights of mountains, admitting two small rivers but no air or coolness. The heat and humidity seemed to gather in trembling waves over the steep jungle-slopes, and all day to roll downward, making of Kuala Lipis a furnace, a nerve-destroying place of dust and silence. Two dozen Malays, a scattering of Chinese, and six white people existed in this valley cauldron.

At daybreak a chorus of dyal birds awakened me, and the distant crow of a wild jungle-cock brought me to my feet with a leap. Then came a dismal clank of iron links, and a half-dozen convicts, all lugging balls and chains, filed up, under an armed Sikh guard, and proceeded to do chambermaid, janitor, and gardener duty. It was an experience worthy of this weird Malay land to have one's room swept by a leering, villainous-mouthed Chinese murderer, with his ball rolling about the floor after him, and getting tangled in bed-legs and chair-legs. Finally, laden with garbage and weeds, the anvil chorus died away in the distance. Later, we saw two members of the gang painfully rolling the tennis-court, carrying their iron balls over their shoulders so as not to damage the court.

I made a short, unsuccessful trip to the jungle, and returned well torn by thorns and with no hint of pheasants heard or seen. Then I called on three white men, made arrangements to go down river on the government houseboat, and was invited to a formal dinner the coming evening. I shall never forget that entertainment—because of its sincere hospitality, its discomfort, and the element of tragedy which ever played and flickered so near the surface. In breathless heat we donned full evening dress, and soon there arrived the half-broken rickshaw which was the only vehicle Kuala Lipis possessed. By dint of one man pulling and another pushing, we accomplished a hundred yards or so, and then had to walk the rest of the way through dense reeds to the house of the Government Agent. The air was still and saturated. Crickets chirped, and once an elephant trumpeted far in the distance. The smoking lantern covered the narrow path with a tapestry of shooting lights and shadows. Once the pulling convict shied, and we stood still while a big black cobra undulated slowly away into the reeds.

We dined on a full-course English dinner, with heating alcoholic drinks, waited on by a quartette of turbaned Indians, with the perspiration pouring down their shining faces. The lamps were gratefully dim, the servants stood silent as ghosts. The atmosphere was tense with an undercurrent of racked nerves. We had heard rumors of nerve-broken men, and we found only four of the six white people to greet us. Something, and something petty and unreasonable, had kept the other man and woman away.

All knew that a deadly epidemic of cholera was surely working its way up river, and preparation for this added to the ghastly climatic and isolated

193

conditions of their daily life. The sight of evening dress brought the memory of the outside world vividly to mind and intensified the terrible trials of this breathless hell. First one, then another, snapped out angrily from time to time, then looked ashamed but never apologized; that would have been to recognize the deadly overwrought nerves, which must not be spoken of. The strain of the breaking-point rose and fell, throbbing like the heat-waves. Once a man smashed in and flatly disputed an assertion. For five minutes there was silence heavy with embarrassment and attempts at control. The only sounds were the pattering of the Malay's feet over the split bamboo, and the squeaking of the punkah-rope, dim jungle sounds, and the rustling of a gecko or snake in the roof. Then I spoke of some casual thing in the outside world, and all leaped hysterically to answer; someone swore at a servant, and again the thread of normal conversation was mended. They begged me to talk, talk, of the coast, of Singapore, of England; but the conversation always settled back to cholera. A woman decided—and changed her mind three times in two courses—to clear out to Kuala Lumpur, then to stick by her husband.

The club was a cheery little building, which gave an impression of coolness that its thermometer refused to second. There were old magazines, an interesting little library, a tennis-court a bit weedy and aslant, and a fifty-yard golf-course, besides an abundance of whiskey and soda-pop. When I visited it next day, I found three Englishwomen —the two who had dined with us the night before, and a third reading by herself.

The third day fever descended quickly upon me, and as the white physicians had gone down river in an attempt to head off the cholera, I sent for the Bengali doctor left in charge of the hospital. He took several hours to dress up in honor of attending a white Sahib, and appeared with hair shining with grease and a collar and necktie, whereas Kuala Lipis etiquette demanded only an undervest. With him he brought a large, black, locked bag, as shining as his hair. From this he took a pair of goggles, and began a series of questions more appropriate to the victim of a census-taker than to a fever-stricken Sahib. I lost patience at this juncture, and demanded a certain definite specific which . my kit lacked. Rather crestfallen, from the very bottom of the bag he fished out the powders I wished, and when he went to mix them, my sense of humor and curiosity overcame my excess of temperature, and I opened the bag and found that it was empty. My specific had exhausted the dusky physician's resources. It was true Bengali philosophy—an inverted Christian Science!

After another day, the Kuala Lipis cauldron began actually to steam; for the monsoon set in and rain came down in torrents all night and was drawn up again through the heated air all day. My fever vanished, and in spite of dismal warnings I got my possessions aboard the tiny houseboat and stretched out full length in my water-line berth, waiting for the retinue of servants-of-all-nations who were at the village bar, absorbing cholera medicine. As I rested, dabbling my hand in the tepid, muddy stream, the houseboat swung out a little, leaving a ribbon of open water between me and the shore. This tiny separation gave me sudden perspective. For the past week I had been in this fever-ridden station and of it. Now, as if the six inches of water which separated us had been as many hundred miles, I saw these splendid British men and women in the true perspective of their terrible isolation: their pluck in preparing for the oncoming fight against cholera, their holding true to the best traditions of their race. I remembered the justice and fairness of government of tiny Indian villages, of Burmese hinterland hamlets, of Sarawak Dyaks, and I thanked God that, next to my own country, I could claim blood-relationship with and loyalty to the other great English-speaking people.

Cleopatra was addicted to houseboating of sorts, and she was supreme in beauty, tact, and courage; houseboating gave freest play to Mark Twain's humor; Moses knew the delights of quiet drifting through reeds and rushes, and great wisdom was his portion. Whenever I go a-houseboating,—and I go whenever I can,—I also attain supremacy— in contentment. Volplaning earthwards from eight-thousand-foot levels, running before a steady breeze in a catamaran—these are smooth, efficient, but tense methods of progress. But to lie in canoe or houseboat and let the current of some stream drift you where it will is a mastery of relaxation. You become a veritable corpuscle in an artery of Mother Earth, one with the drifting leaves all about, and a worthy member of the little company which acquires merit at the shrine of kindly Jabim.

When tearing across the face of the earth in a train, or surging ahead in a great steamer, I usually have a boding feeling of finality: this little farmhouse or that crow-dotted clump of trees I shall surely never see again; the distant island must be dropping irrevocably below the horizon. Drifting, however, engenders a peculiarly optimistic frame of mind; I am complacently confident of coming cycles; I am conscious of a close spiral of reincarnation. Like the drops of water which support and drift with me, I pass mighty tacubas and fallen trees, masses of brilliant bloom and peering monkeys, with a satisfied conviction that, like the drops of water, I shall again return to drift down this stream, and again rejoice in all its beauty and mystery.

So, when my motley crew was gathered, I gave Matsam, the Malay captain, orders to drift, not paddle. But even when the six inches of open water between boat and shore had increased to as many yards, I found that I was still within the British sphere of kindly influence, and the District Officer ran down and tossed across to me a big green hand-grenade-looking thing, shouting that he had just picked it from his garden—the biggest cucumber ever grown in Malaysia.

If there was a Lloyd's rating of houseboats, my craft would occupy an intermediate position. It was far superior to an ark of bulrushes, daubed with slime and pitch; but, on the other hand, it was not of beaten gold, or provided either with silver oars, or purple, perfumed sails. But the Strander, as I called it, from its chief occupation, had a jolly little cabin amidships, with storeroom and kitchen aft, and men's deck and paddling-space forward. Overhead was a tiny awninged nook just large enough for a steamer-chair; while high over the storeroom sat the captain, with a tiller-end which wandered aimlessly but effectively down and back to a rudder far below.

My cabin was a magic cabin; and just as magicians of old wrought their spells by necromantic passes, so I controlled the metamorphosis of my cabin by posture. When I lay in my bunk it was bedroom, when I sat up, my head boy Aladdin wafted in a tiny table from somewhere, and it became dining-room. With the curtains lowered, I stood and leaned over my various trays and graduates, and my cabin became dark-room. And finally, when my rookha chair was brought and an erring member of the crew summoned, the dignity of a court-room descended upon the lowly little place.

So began days of drifting, and never in my experience was a crew more enthusiastic about a mode of travel. Only for occasional meals and more frequent strandings did they break their slumber. One of them I doomed to stand continual watch because he snored unpleasantly. I could not find the Malay word for snore, so to this day he never knows why I picked on him. An extra allowance of pay, however, palliated my linguistic ignorance. Even if I could have made my motive clear, I should have been in difficulty; for another paddler also snored, but in a minor, inoffensive key, his timbre and rhythm partaking of the quality of natural sounds around us. In fact, for several days I mistook his ronflement for the sound of a gentle wind, or water rippling beneath the bow.

Day after day I drifted down the Jelai, sometimes stranding on a sandbar, which would be so interesting that I spent the day. At evening we would tie up to an overhanging branch beyond the reach of mosquitos and leeches, and swing slowly at the hest of wind and current. In the heart of one of the wildest regions of the world, with elephants and tigers, fierce black leopards, and equally dangerous wild cattle in the surrounding forest, it was a joy to lie in pyjamas full length in my bunk in the cool air, dabbling my hand in the water, and listening to the night sounds of the Malay jungle. My dabbling was intermittent and rather conscious, and always on the shore side of the boat, for crocodiles were too abundant in mid-stream to permit of carelessness, although I had just taken a plunge and a good swim.

PHEASANT JUNGLES

I clapped twice, and my Cinghalese boy Aladdin appeared with a lime-squash; and as I sipped it, I thought of envious friends at home. But I wondered how many of them would have enjoyed earning this luxurious hour by the day's tramp through swamps, crawling through leech-infested thorn thickets, with heat and gnats and crackling leaves hindering the noiseless approach to a flock of peafowl, or a solitary argus, or a family of peacock pheasants. Only aching muscles and excited memory of new facts achieved could make perfect the enjoyment of such an evening.

From the front of the boat came the sound of low, minor singing, my Malay paddlers droning weird falsetto songs or sleepily chanting proverbs in turn. A great fish, perhaps crocodile-chased, leaped frantically into the air, so close that a shower of drops fell on me. From a long distance away came two sounds, low and of short duration, but powerful in their appeal to the imagination: the brazen trumpet of an elephant and the penetrating cry of a male argus pheasant on its dancing ground. Then arose a muffled, palpitating series of vocal waves, which rolled in, rising higher, clearing to a crisp utterance, and finally reaching the full swell and power of a rollicking chorus of wa-was or gibbons—great ape-like monkeys which fill the Malay jungles with the exuberance of their emotions.

No imaginable sound would seem less fitted to the wilderness—it was so unsophisticated, so youthful, so full of joy and laughter. It recalled the words of Dunsany's frightened Man: "Rock should not walk. . . . Rock should not walk in the evening." And here in my swaying houseboat I listened and said over and over again, "Children should not laugh in the jungle.—They should not laugh in the jungle at night."

At last the wa-was died down to a low, sleepy mumbling, with now and then an individual, ringing, staccato whoop, like the final dying flares of the fire-music. Soothed and rested, I turned over and had almost found slumber, when I heard a suspicious swashing forward. I sat up, reached for the electric light which lay with my revolver, and leaning far out over the water, suddenly flashed it along the boat. There was the villainous China-boy cook in sharp silhouette, washing a handful of forks, knives, and spoons in the river. I leaned back and clapped for Aladdin.

"Bring cookie, lantern, pail of boiling water, dishes."

"Going, marster."

Cookie appeared and salaamed, rather yellow-white and trembling; Aladdin's eyes were big with excitement.

"I told him always cook spoons." (Aladdin always allied himself with the side of right early in any dramatic situation.)

"On your knees, cookie, and wash each fork carefully in boiling water." (This he had been told to do at the beginning of the trip.)

"If ever not do so again, will throw overboard to crocodiles."

Cookie, whiter, mumbles to Aladdin, who whispers officiously aside, "Tink will never do again, marster" (as one Supreme Court Justice confers with another).

Each night afterward, however, there occurred the rite of "visible spoon-washing." Often I would not be there, but would come in from the jungle to find cookie on his knees washing to an empty cabin; and once, coming softly, I surprised Aladdin, sitting in my rookha chair, receiving the obeisance of the ritual in solemn state. He was extolling "Marster's" lenience in not throwing cookie to the crocodiles; so I pretended not to see him, and, coughing, gave him a chance to seem making ready the bed for the night, although the clothes were already turned down.

With dead cholera victims floating past, and down river two hundred cases out of every two hundred dying, I dared take no risk. Our drink was the universal Japanese mineral water Tan-san, or thrice-boiled river water.

Another evening and its following day—the day of peacocks—stand out even among a month of wonderful Malay days. We tied up in some unknown reach of the Pahang on a moonless evening, when men came softly and, talking to my boatmen, wished to be hired. I needed some extra help, so called ashore to engage three. Before I slept I looked out and tried to pierce the blackness; but the jungle rose, a solid wall of jet, sending to my strained senses only an occasional fragrant wave of perfume from nocturnal blossoms, a shrill monotone of insect, or the sinister sighing of some small animal. Once a half-submerged tree drifted past, scraping the sides with its withered foliage, and flicking off a beautiful tree-cricket, which awakened me by crawling over my face. After its capture the night passed quietly.

To wake in a tent, open the flaps, and look out is good; to sit up in one's blanket cocoon in a hammock and see the jungle dawn is better; but best of all is opening one's eyes in a houseboat bunk, and without further movement seeing water and jungle and sky, and the exciting early morning doings of fish, crocodiles, birds, and monkeys. One feels as yet unburdened with a human frame; and for an hour I am only a pair of disembodied eyes, which search and record, begrudging even the interruption of winks, and viewing all through fresh-colored, sidewise vision.

As one wakes slowly from slumber, so came the dawn, gradually, in these tropical lowlands. The glare of the sudden leap of the sun above the horizon was dimmed, delayed, diluted, by the thick morning mist—mist whose grayness I loved to think of as the exact shade of "elephant's breath." As I looked out over the side of the boat, the swift current became more and more distinct through the fog, which drifted slowly downward like a sluggish, aerial river flowing gently over the denser one below. When the light grew and the mist lifted and frayed upward, a brown line quartered the fore-glow in the sky and masses of foliage took shape and color beyond the sand-banks. Here and there white-barked trunks gleamed like ghosts, the satu-rated air was heavy with the odor of plume-blos-soms, and the eddies were filled with their petals. A pair of great hornbills crossed high overhead, hidden by cloud-mist, but registering every wing-beat in a loud, deep, *whoof! whoof!* Bulbuls burst into song, drongos sent down their hoarse cries from the tree-tops, with showers of drops which pattered on my cabin roof.

Another veil of mist was drawn aside, and I sat up, breathless and tense, for on a sand-bar up-river and up-wind four great black forms became dimly visible—giant, statuesque sladang, the big-gest bull standing at least six feet at the shoulder. Even against the pale sand their cream-colored stockings showed clearly, and their magnificent curved horns lay far back as they stood with nostrils outstretched toward me, striving to make out by sight what the wind refused to explain. We seemed harmless—some huge tree stranded during the night; but with wilderness folk, vague suspicion is interpreted as proven danger, and the wonderful jungle cattle, still headed our way, moved slowly through the shallows around and behind an arm of foliage.

The other end of the sand-bar held for me even greater interest. Resting my stereo glasses on the edge of the bunk, I was fairly in the midst of five green peafowl. They had me under surveillance, but were too confident of their powers to think of leaving. Two had sweeping trains which cleared the damp sand as they walked. Now and then a bird stood quite erect and flapped his wings vigorously, to rid the feathers of excess of moisture. I could even see the others shake their heads as the drops flew over them. Two young of the year were very active, running about, chasing one another, or stopping to scratch among the gravel.

A passing log drew the attention of the peafowl, and they all stood motionless, watching it, until they were certain it was wood, not crocodile. The sun shone brightly for a moment, and the mists swirled away, showing distant hills. Peal after peal of rollicking laughter came from a family of serious-faced wa-was. Then a rush of wind and fog blotted out the sun, and a sudden shower pitted the smooth water. From the depths of this renewed twilight rang the piercing, unrestrained cry of wild peacock; and when I rolled over my bunk edge, plunged in and swam swiftly to the bar, I found only tracks—cloven and tripartite—to hint of the rare vision which this fortunate dawn offered to me.

Returning, I clapped for breakfast and prepared for a long day's matching of my poor senses and wood-craft against those of the wary peafowl. I went ashore and was balancing my ammunition, when a face suddenly appeared, more horrible than any beast, more inhuman than the lowest monkey. It was but the memory of a face, and should have belonged to a corpse long since buried; but, instead, it surmounted a living, well-made body. Then I saw three men, and realized that I had engaged, "sight unseen," three lepers. I gave them money and food and sent them on their way swiftly, with Aladdin to escort them well beyond the limits of our explorations—a duty over which he was not enthusiastic.

This horrible shock, together with a brief return of fever, made that forenoon a nerve-fashioned mirage. I felt the change as soon as I was within the hot, steaming shade. The heat and humidity pressed upon me like material substances. I listened, yet dreaded to hear sounds, fearing them only less than the endless silence which framed them. When I squatted on a log, the rhythm of the host of advancing leeches would sometimes seem to merge into a thousand endless, undulating lines of vermin, closing in on all sides, and the feel of their measured loopings on neck or wrist or hat-rim was almost unendurable. The windless shush, shush, of leaves under their combined movement increased, until it became a veritable bellowing. Once I stood up and fired both barrels of my gun into the tree-tops, and for a while my mind cleared. Then I watched a small python stalking a lizard—watched without interest, until I realized that I was observing a real tragedy and not a heat-induced mirage of the mind.

I longed to return, but knew I must not. I could not give in to this terror of jungle things which usually aroused only interest. Then came the climax. I had the chance of my life,—ten peacocks at close range,—and for a while was pulling myself together, when I fairly screamed and dropped my gun, leaping from my hiding-place and climbing ten feet into a tree tenanted by fire-ants, in a trembling sweat of fear. A tiny squirrel —one of the little dwarfs scarcely as long as one's hand—had jumped on my back, and I had reacted as from the charge of a buffalo.

The fever seemed simultaneously to have broken, and although weak and dizzy, I set out to achieve something definite before I gave in and returned to my bunk. The peacocks, at my outcry, had taken refuge in distant, tall dead trees, high above the jungle; and clearing my neck and ankles of the abominable leeches, I began a stalk. I shifted my firing lever to the third, a rifle-barrel, and changed the .303 soft-nose to a steel-jacket. Only occasionally could I see my bird, a beauty in full plumage, who shared the bleached, lightning-struck giant with a trio of courting drongos. I dared not approach too close, and the last twenty yards I crept forward from the blind side, from which the bird's head was hidden by a splintered branch. When I first aimed, the gun-barrel wavered like wheat in the wind; but after sitting quietly for a few moments, I felt myself steadying, thought of lime-squashes to come, and fired. The

bird leaped a yard or two into the air, then spread
wings and train and came down in a veritable tail-
spin which awoke shuddering memories. Marking
down the compass direction, I stepped heedlessly
forward and went myself into a nose-dive of sorts.
I fell and fell, and ended in a shower of sparks of
physical pain. I had stepped off the edge of a
sheer bank into a hidden gully, and hung suspended
in mid-air in a cruel netting of rotan thorns. There
was still eight feet more to solid ground, and for
fifteen memorable minutes I was the plaything of
gravitation and all the needle-thorns in the world.
Every strand of barbed wire which I cut would
gain me a few inches of descent and a score more
scratches. I could only defend my eyes with hand-
kerchief-wrapped hand, as I descended that awful
round of purgatory, and rested at last, leech-re-
gardless, on the wet moss.

Retrieving my gun, I was fortunate enough to
find my bird on the second circle cast; and taking
it under my arm, with the jeweled train streaming
far behind, I trudged slowly back. I am sure that
old-fashioned cupping and bleeding must have miraculous powers, for between the leeches and the
thorns I had been thoroughly treated, and no ill
effects followed. The following day I had to rest;
but when again I made my way through this same
jungle, I saw it only as a place of wonder, of keen
delight, and of deepest interest.

Rest-House at Semangko Pas, Pahang

My House-Boat on the Jelai River, Selangor

Camping on the Balleh River, Sarawak, Borneo

VIII

It was late afternoon in the heart of the great island of Borneo. I had tramped all day through the jungle and now, at the very end of my trek, had located what I thought was an old dancing arena of an argus pheasant, on a hillock only fifty yards from the bank of the Mujong River. I walked on, located my tiny dug-out, and ridding myself of my jungle-hued clothing, slipped over the gunwale into the dark chocolate waters. In and out of the overhanging roots I swam, every pore of me drinking in the coolness. I clung to a half-submerged vine and let the current sway me back and forth, and searching with my eyes for a chirping insect on an old fallen tree near by I suddenly saw close to my face a six foot serpent coiled on a branch which still kept its bark above water. I did not recognize it, but it was manifestly a "hot snake" as my Dyak interpreter called poisonous species. I thought how exactly this scene would typify the deadly tropics to my stay-at-home friends. And yet here I was swimming amid the shadows of a strange tropic river, with a venomous serpent watching me, and was probably quite as safe from harm as I would have been in any mill-

209

pond at home. In such a pond a snapping turtle might, in the realm of possibilities, amputate a toe or a foot, or it is far from inconceivable that a rattlesnake or a copperhead might be coiled under my clothing on the bank; I might have to climb out through a mass of poison ivy and in my progress disturb a wasp's nest.

The serpent and I watched each other for a time with respectful interest and then I swam back to my craft and drifted slowly down stream toward the great war canoe which was my present home. When within a few bends of it I drew myself beneath a maze of branches and lianas and watched the day die over the brown Bornean waters.

Straight down stream the sun was hidden in a blaze of yellow and gold clouds before it sank, resulting in an unusually long tropic twilight. Then an afterglow tinted the eastern clouds high over the upper Mujong, violet and pale wine color. The two banks of the river became darker, duskier green, and finally all but the sky-mirrored outermost leaves changed to black. The sky was pale blue; the muddy water a nameless, beautiful brown. The banks were lifeless most of the day, the jungle folk keeping to the inner forests. Now, however, in the cool of early evening, birds' voices were heard. Small flocks of fruit pigeons dashed over the trees, large mynas perched on tall plum trees, and a family of gibbons shook the branches of a tree in the distance. In a black concavity of the pale, clayey bank a lighter spot appeared, framed by bushes. My glasses showed a wild boar, fore-feet stamping, tushes gnashing and twisted tail flicking. Had he not been against the blackest shadow he would have been invisible, as he was coated with the mud of the banks. The flies gave him no peace, and he soon turned and climbed awkwardly into the dark jungle behind. The first flying fox of the evening now appeared, flapping slowly and gracefully as a heron, and by turns soaring like a pelican; then a score of these giant, five-foot bats came into sight, high in air. As the mynas flew from their trees to some distant roost, the bats swung up to the clusters of fruit and enveloped them like starfishes on oysters, swinging around head downward and eating away with all their might. They take the place, in flight along the rivers, of herons, of which I saw none in Borneo. A brace of bluish ducks larger than teal flew across the river, and distant shrills announced the evening concert of the great five o'clock cicadas.

Then came unannounced, the sight of sights. A few paces to the right of the wild boar's wallow, my eye caught a movement against the water-washed bare face of clay. Fortunately I was looking along the tops of the barrels of my glasses, a habit of mine when locating anything by eyesight, the finding of which requires instant but inconspicuous adjustment of the lenses. I pushed them up into focus and there sprang into clear-cut delineation what my eyes had refused to separate from the shadows of the bank,—a male argus pheasant drinking from a rain pool a yard or more from the moiled current of the river. It was half crouched, and the motion of the head, alternately raised and lowered, was all that betrayed the bird. The long wings, the gracefully twisted tail-feathers were as motionless as if carved in cameo against the earthern bank. I watched it thus for a minute, two minutes, then my attention wandered for a moment to some creature near at hand, and when I looked back the bird was just disappearing. I had seen my first wild argus, brief though the glimpse had been.

Then in the dusk there passed on the stream a little miniature boat, floating uncertainly along, carefully carven, with many little figures standing bravely up, looking woodenly toward their fate in the distant sea. This was the work of native Dyaks, who prepare them with the greatest care when a family is attacked with illness, and set them free, hoping the bad spirit will accompany these "doubles" of the afflicted. These little spirit craft have been washed ashore as far away as Singapore.

The stars burned out brightly and the wet mists of night settled down before I followed the little Dyak boat and drifted around the last bend into sight of my giant canoe. On the beach were my dozen native paddlers and their fire lit up the circle of great bronze bodies—a wild sight in this wild country. The light also was reflected from the long, low, thatched canoe shelter which was my home.

WITH THE DYAKS OF BORNEO

In my search for the pheasants of Borneo I had left Kuching, and acting on the advice of Rajah Brooke, had penetrated far into the interior of Sarawak. One hundred and fifty miles up the Rejang I entered the Balleh, and at Kapit, the uttermost outpost, I obtained the great war canoe which I was now using. With thirteen paddlers I made my way up the Mudyong, a river which has its origin on the very slopes of Mount Tjemaroe in Dutch territory.

This present stop was temporary, in order that I might be sure that we were in the country of the great ruoi or argus. Now that I had actually seen one, I planned in the morning to move on up stream and there find a suitable place where I could shoot, watch and study at leisure as many of the five Bornean pheasants as possible.

After I had slept for an hour a distant peal of thunder awoke me. Wind and rain followed and I peered out through the mat curtains to see the Dyaks climbing aboard with all the things which had been taken ashore. They also loosened the ropes that tied us to the trunks of trees. I dozed for a while longer and then the storm broke. Down river it came, and the water descended in floods. The river was churned into a white froth, the whole surface being covered with swirling eddies of muddy foam. In the glare of lightning these looked singularly menacing as they creamed up along the sides of the boat—appearing so solid, yet moving so silently and swiftly with the current.

PHEASANT JUNGLES

The roof of the rattan cabin was tight and only near the ends did I have to shift my guns and cameras. My fellow voyageurs in the bottom of the great dugout did not fare so well, and soon several lines of ants appeared, climbing up in panic, carrying their eggs and infants to the safe dryness of my sleeping compartment. There being an abundance of room for us all I did not disturb them, and they made three separate piles of their treasures. Early next morning when the canoe was bailed out they took up their nurseries and vanished.

Looking out during a particularly vivid flash of lightning I saw that the bank had disappeared, and supposed that we had drifted down stream. Later as the storm increased, I realized that we had moved only upward, and were among the lower branches. A canoe passed at the height of the storm. From the wild outcries of the Dyaks, the unsteady flourishing of half-extinguished torches, and the uncertain guidance of the craft I knew that they had come from some bacchanalian feast. In the bow stood a magnificent naked figure of a man, fending off floating trees. A zigzag streak of lightning outlined him sharply as though carved in jet—showing his tattooing, his gold ornaments and the hornbill feathers in his headdress. Then the blackness of the storm swallowed him up.

Throughout the night my Dyaks never ceased their skilful manipulation of the craft. In the dazzling flashes I could see that the storm had made

214

Chief Coe

A savage Dyak, intelligent, gentle, with caste

One of My Paddlers

A kindly soul, whose whole face was distorted by desperate near-sightedness

Narok, the Dancer

a veritable liquid avalanche of the river; in the darkness great tree-trunks rushed past, and at times it seemed as if nothing could save the canoe from being cut in two. The next flash showed a row of heads like a moving cordon in the water surrounding the boat. Now and then a hand and arm were lifted to fend off some debris, or a sword gleamed and a menacing branch was lopped off. When I caught the eye of Drojak or of Djamwhak a broad grin greeted me, sometimes smothered by the slapping of an unexpected creamy wave. It was a memorable night and in the early dawn I saw that we were tethered to the topmost branches of the tree to whose trunk we had been moored the night before. The river had risen twenty-five feet in these few hours, and without the unceasing lopping of branches, the constant easing out and shifting of the tremendously long, narrow canoe, we would have been caught and overturned by the first branch encountered in our upward progress. The men took to their paddles after breakfast as if they had slept soundly all night.

When at last I chose a place for a permanent camp the Dyaks put up a series of palm thatched shelters in an incredibly short time. At one end was the laundry, consisting of the river, a stone on which to pound clothes and a jungle vine on which to dry them. At the other end was the zoo,—always a noisy and exciting place. Between was the raised bamboo platform on which I ate, on which Cookie Mutt served delicious hot dishes, and from which

Din-din, my Dyak boy, snatched the half-finished meal if I so much as looked up at a passing bird. For in his opinion, to cease eating for a moment was to be through. Next was the Dyak Hotel, a palm shelter where my paddlers and hunters rested and smoked and entertained visiting savages, and where they discussed endlessly my incomprehensible trip and ways, in guttural, banjo-twanging syllables. The last wall-less room was the largest, and combined laboratory, photographer's shop, writing room, museum and doctor's office. Here were my specimens and here came a succession of sick savages for treatment, most of them beyond permanent help, to be sent away filled with false hopes aroused by morphine relief.

The most ingenious bit of architecture was the elevated, bamboo viaduct which led from the great dugout over the yards of quaking mud to the bank. In the nightly storms this was sometimes a yard or two under water, but when washed off next day was as serviceable a path as ever.

I have elsewhere told of the individualization of Umar as money-lender in chief to Tuan, and this automatically made every one of my Dyaks a pronounced personality. Before, I had sometimes been at a loss to tell one from another; they had not been long with me, and it is easier to consider many people as a crowd and to estimate them accordingly, than to set apart each unit and judge it alone. However, through the indirect grace of Umar, it was not long before we became friends.

WITH THE DYAKS OF BORNEO

These Dyaks, unlike the Cinghalese, showed interest in the work at hand and lent themselves readily to whatever task called for their help. They had no idea what I wanted with pheasants, but they loved the hunt and were eager to put all their knowledge and skill at the service of Burong-orang, the bird-man. Science was an abstraction far beyond their experience and imagination, but they speculated among themselves on my motives and the underlying purpose of the trip. They saw the bodies often thrown away, and as often retrieved them even when they had achieved the superlative of highness as game goes;—plainly food was not my object. Some were certain that the feathers and bones were to be used as medicine, or at any rate were to be sold, in time, for some indefinite purpose. Others held, and these were in the majority, that the feathers were to be used for head-dresses. I was tracking head-dresses through the marshes and the jungle, and some day, at some auspicious hour, I would take them back to the white man's land,—for myself and other men to wear. For it goes without saying that such things are not for women.

These Dyaks could build a camp or break it with great speed and thoroughness. They were superior woodsmen, and knew what was necessary about the jungle. They would follow or they would wait at the signal, and they asked no questions. But they would look wistfully at my gun when game came within sight, and their faces would be troubled and overcast when I elected to watch and not to shoot. At night, about the campfires, they talked about this, rehearsed all that had taken place, expressing a gentle indignation and a profound wonder. A bush would represent the ruoi or argus, the semp-idan or fire-backed pheasant which I had hunted; a blow-pipe, my gun. I would see them sometimes absorbed in this drama. Finally, when I asked about it, I learned that it had been decided that I was an unaccountable hunter, but that they respected whatever I chose to do, since it was evident that I, like themselves, was governed by signs and by omens. Doubtless, the shooting of my pheasants was no light matter, and if a white butterfly crossed my path at the moment the burong appeared, then Tuan was more than justified in saving his fire. In this tolerance, in this withholding of judgment, I saw what was finest in the Dyak character. What they did not understand they did not therefore condemn. Would that many tourists and some explorers could learn from them.

As for Cookie, he could not conceal his contempt for these foolish superstitions. Eking out his very scanty English with Malay words, he would hold forth at length on the colossal absurdity of an entire village tearing up its houses and moving elsewhere because a certain sunbird alighted on a certain spot at a certain time. Very, very bad, was Cookie's verdict, when all the world knows that the success of house-building depends wholly on the moon— that fatal moon of madness—and that there are, at best, but three proper days in the calendar for moving.

But there was one Dyak in the crew about whom Cookie had little to say. This was Drojak, the gentlest and kindliest of all the great savages in Borneo, who worked for the success of the trip with patience and loyalty. It happened one morning when far away from the camp that Drojak was attacked by twelve men from a Dutch tribe. When he returned from this encounter, eight heads were hanging from his girdle. He said little about the matter, but from that hour he was no longer Drojak, paddler, but Drojak-no-spear-can-touch-him. He was a quiet, slow-thinking man who liked to sit in silence watching the camp-fire, where the light played over his dark skin and turned it to bronze, and made two little bright spots of flame when it touched the heavy brass earrings which hung almost to his shoulders. But, at rare intervals, he could be persuaded to re-enact the fight which had brought him his new native name. Then his quickness was marvellous, his hands and his arms moved faster than the eye, every lunge and thrust was the very essence of savagery.

He was a great actor and his audience would wait in absolute silence watching him. And the audience was as picturesque as it was appreciative,—my Malay cook, superstitious and filled with awe at such a sight, Matelly, Umar, Din-din and eleven Dyak paddlers and hunters. They would sit in a half circle about the camp fire, with the Malay hovering fearfully in the background. I was always given a place of honor a little at one side. Behind us, the jungle rose like a black wall, and beyond the camp fire the river reflected its higher flames in watery lightnings.

First Drojak would walk slowly up and down, showing tall and black against the yellow flames, wearing only his narrow loin cloth, and the long brass ear-rings. This was the prelude—an imitation of the way he had walked through the forest on the morning of his battle. Then he would stop, peer cautiously from side to side, lean forward listening. He would give quickly, with gestures, with short, broken, twanging words, the advance of his enemy—the advance of twelve men creeping toward him through the thick underbrush. Then, with his sword raised above his head—the same carven, hair-decorated weapon which hangs before me in my studio—how he had run out to meet the enemy. He would show the ugly details of the fight, how first one man went down before him, and how another body was thrown across the first, and how he stabbed a third in the back, when he had tripped over a root. We knew how each of these men had died, one with his hands held up before his face, another with his hands caught behind him and his head pressed down. Luck and accident and chance must have aided him as well as his own strength and agility, which were greater than I have ever seen combined in any one man. Otherwise such unfair odds would have been hopeless.

Dancing Arena of the Argus Pheasant

Wives of Dyak Chief at Whose House I was Entertained

WITH THE DYAKS OF BORNEO

There were times, I think, when Drojak forgot that we were watching him. At such moments his face was terrible to see, filled with cruelty and hate. But I believe that his battle was fought honorably, according to his codes. Twelve men trailed him, attacked him. It was a question of his life. He killed eight of them and drove four of them back into the forest. It must have been, by any standards of warfare, a magnificent battle. My mind kept going back to the last fight of Umslopagaas.

He showed us how the four ran away, how one of them threw his spear into a clump of bushes, where it fell, point downward, so that it struck deep into the ground. It remained upright, swaying a little from side to side. Such minor details gave to his whole recountal the stamp of truth. He showed us, too, the way he had cut off the heads of his enemies, and we could not mistake his hint that two were not quite dead. Then, in pantomime, he tied them one after another to his belt, quietly, deliberately, taking great pains with each knot. One apparently came undone and rolled a little way downhill before he recovered it.

At the end he would straighten up, put back his shoulders, and wipe his hands. The deep lines around his mouth and his forehead would disappear suddenly. Then he would look at his audience in a manner that I could never explain, turning slowly from one face to another until he had completed the half circle. This done, he would put his feet together so that his heels touched, straighten up and burst into a hearty laugh.

There was something contagious about his laughter. It was so loud and so genuine. And it was without fail the signal for Mutt, the Cookie, to reappear from the bushes where he took refuge during the second act of Drojak's drama. For the Malay sometimes became arrogant over his cooking pots—and criticized the customs of the Dyaks rather openly. And he seemed to find much food for thought when he saw Drojak killing so many men single-handed before the fire. I believe he did not like the light in Drojak's eyes, and once when it was all over, and Drojak playfully made as though to throw his spear in Mutt's direction, he took refuge behind me and in hoarse whispers and absolutely unintelligible Malay expressed himself to himself—doubtless his forcible opinion of Dyak humor.

As the days passed I wished them weeks, and when they became weeks I longed to extend them to months. It took all my junglesmanship to ferret out the secrets of the pheasants—shooting them was the easiest part. And always I was tempted to turn aside to the fascinating trails of other birds, animals, reptiles and insects.

Borneo is a land of flying creatures, and besides birds, bats and insects, I saw squirrels, lizards, frogs and even snakes occasionally trusting themselves to the thin air, buoying themselves or at least breaking their fall, with parachutes or membranes of fur, skin or scales. One of the most interesting and beautiful is a large furry creature, somewhat squirrel-like in general appearance, which has unfortunately no correct common name. It is usually known as the flying lemur but this is no more applicable than the literal translation of its scientific name *Galeopithecus volans*—the flying weasel-monkey, for it is neither one nor the other of these animals, but rather a distant cousin of moles and shrews. But here again it presents the anomaly of being classed with the insectivores while in diet it is a vegetarian.

Now and then I would see one in an open glade or old trail of the Bornean jungle between five in the afternoon and dusk. A large dark mass would detach itself unexpectedly from high up on the trunk of a tree and pass with a rush close to my face in a smooth, gliding flight to another tree, perhaps forty yards or more away. From the general aspect and noiseless flight, I thought, when I first saw one of these nocturnal animals, that it was some large owl making a low swoop through the glade. But I marked the spot where it alighted, and creeping up I saw a large, flat, irregularly draped figure, topped with a fox-like head glued to the vertical trunk. I later found that the flying lemurs show two distinct color phases, a rufous and a grey, like screech owls, quite independent of age or sex. The rufous phase was in my experience much rarer, characterizing only about one in every dozen individuals.

PHEASANT JUNGLES

I am probably the only person who ever collected a baby flying lemur on a bicycle. I was riding from the Kuching Museum to my dâk bungalow late one evening, when something suddenly struck me full on the chest, almost unseating me. Instantly the something flopped off, and not until I had ridden on for a few minutes did I realize that a smaller something still clung to my woolen shirt. I stopped and found that a mother lemur had evidently swooped accidentally against me, and in the sudden collision had dislodged her baby, which had been clinging to her, and which was now crouched closely against me uttering a low rasping cry. Another youngster which I salvaged from a tree-top, lived for a few days, but it would not feed satisfactorily so I chloroformed it. None have ever been brought alive out of Borneo.

Hidden deep beneath the surface of the ground in the Bornean jungles are thousands of great reptile-like creatures, some fully six feet long, covered from nose to tail-tip with a complete armature of scales; lizards in appearance, mammals in truth, orphans in relationship. The first pangolin I ever saw my Dyaks and I dug out of a burrow near camp. The name sounds more like a musical instrument than an animal, but in reality it has been twisted by Anglo-Saxon tongues from the native takjiling. Under his armor of scales the pangolin or scaly anteater conceals a bodily structure as confusing to the scientist as is his general appearance to the layman. In common with other toothless or nearly toothless devourers of ants, the pangolin has usually been classed with armadillos and hairy anteaters. But his structure is so peculiarly pangolinian, his resemblance to other living creatures so slight, and the absence of fossil relatives so complete, that he has finally been assigned to a special order of his own—Pholidota.

Throughout the days of violent sunshine or tropical downpours not one of the host of pangolins ever shows himself; but in the dusk of evening the round, shingled ball stirs in its underground chamber, unrolls, stretches, and the earth gives up its race of scaly anteaters. They come forth timidly, hesitating long at the entrance of the burrow before daring to shuffle forth on their quest for food. The lizard appearance is, as I have said, only a superficial resemblance. The helmet of the deep-sea diver recalls the helm of the medieval knight; yet one is intended as a protection against a yielding liquid, the other to withstand the blows of metal. In the unborn pangolin the scales are little more than a mass of felted hairs, which harden after birth.

The world of night into which the pangolin enters is a world of conflict and fear; there is food in abundance, fruit, berries, mice, sleeping birds at hand, or there are hosts of larger creatures to be overcome and devoured. But the scaly one asks nothing of these. Peace to go his way, a populous ant-hill and a burrow to which to return—this plumbs the depths of a pangolin's desire. His armor is for defense alone, his muscles impel no offensive blows, his powerful claws are only his implements of trade, the picks of a sapper and miner.

The last heave of my shovel rolled my pangolin out upon the forest floor as inanimate as a glacier-worn boulder in a New England field, or like some gigantic, malformed pine cone. There was absolutely no vulnerable point of attack. A rounded back dwindled gradually into a long tapering tail, with part of a hind leg to fill up every intervening crevice. The tail muscles were as rigid as steel. Even with the spade and a Dyak's sword as leverage hardly an inch of the perfect circle could be disturbed. From the jaws of a leopard the scaly ball would have slipped harmlessly away.

Left quiet for five minutes, the only sign of life was the lifting of some of the leaf-like scales of the hip. One imagined that there might be eyes beneath; in such a strange creature any weird distribution of the sense of sight would be credible. This raising of the scales proved to be in the nature of a trick, an invitation to a waiting enemy. Any attempt to seize one of those temptingly lifted scales resulted in disaster; like the jaws of a steel trap they snapped down with such force as to bruise the finger cruelly, or actually to pinch off a bit of flesh. One's enthusiasm for scientific investigation in this direction was satiated at one trial, which was also sufficient to prove Bergson's

Drojak-No-Spear-Can-Touch-Him

Pangolin, or Scaly Anteater, Rolled Up

Pangolin Walking

theory of humor and laughter applicable to Dyaks as having its basis in cruel lack of sympathy.

If the second setting of the scale trap in the succeeding few minutes remained unsprung, the next sign of the evolution of the pangolin was the gradual drawing forth of his head, always with his fore-paws held tightly across his face just below his eyes, like a boy cheating at blind man's buff. The little dull eyes looked around, then the long, mobile snout came into play with its much keener sense of smell, and the ears with their sense, the most valuable of all to this animal. If the coast seemed clear, the tail swung around, the short legs gathered themselves together and the creature ambled off. With such perfection of defense, flight is needless, so his fastest gait is a man's slow walk. And his normal position on the march is very unlike that conceived and executed by the average museum taxidermist. His tail drags, his head is held low and his back is steeply arched, reminding one of the old Stegosaurus of Jurassic days. Swift flight is indeed as impossible as it would be for a man in full medieval armor.

The pangolin is made for ants, and ants alone; without them he would starve at once; with a goodly supply it is difficult to conceive of his dying, except from old age or overeating. The mouth is tiny, as only ants pass in, the tongue is very long, serpent-like in its mobility and covered with glutinous saliva. Why it does not englue as much earth as ants it is hard to explain. To attempt to subsist on the ants found wandering about the forest would be like harvesting wheat grain by grain, so it is necessary for the pangolin to go to the metropolis for supplies. This is almost the most important work of its life and we find it admirably adapted for this. Twenty very strong claws, backed by muscles of immense power, suffice to tear through the ant-hills, hard almost as concrete. It can neither ensheath its claws like a cat, nor carry them raised above the ground like the screamer, so it folds them back, doubled up like jack-knives, beneath the soles of its feet, and thus walks upon them, the edges and the points being kept unblunted.

Home is a chamber at the end of an underground tunnel. Occasionally a pangolin achieves Nirvana by burrowing into a giant ant-hill and there sleeps away his days and eats away his nights, until death relieves him of the sheer monotony of living. Such an accusation may be unjust however, for in common with all organic beings, his safety and nourishment are but means to an end, and to continue his race he must find a mate.

Ants, both stinging and harmless, form his entire food, although we must extend this general term to include the neuropterous termites or white ants. I have counted five hundred fire-ants in the gizzard of a pangolin, their bites and stings powerless against the sticky, merciless tongue which played and played again amongst them, each time sweeping away scores. Lacking teeth, the pangolin swallows tiny pebbles which, as in a chicken, aid in crushing the hard bodies of the ants.

My temporary zoo in camp, besides the flying lemur and the pangolin, contained other beings quite as strange. I gathered many specimens of the pheasants, including the almost unknown white-tailed wattled, as well as exquisite little wood partridges, giant cuckoos and brilliant, rainbow-hued pittas. At one time we were the rather embarrassed owners of a leopard, and there was mutual relief when he escaped during a nocturnal storm. In other cages were zebra civet cats, tupaias or tree-shrews, mouse-deer, spiny rats and porcupines. A white moon-rat was one of the most astonishing, and when this escaped the excitement rose to boiling pitch. The Dyaks were proud of this capture and determined that it should not get away, and the general result must have closely resembled Drojak's battle with twelve men. A dozen naked Dyaks leaped and ran and tumbled and yelled, splashing into the shallows or squdging through the mud to head off the poor creature, others waving blow-pipes and swords from the jungle side, until at last the moon-rat in uttermost despair ran back into its cage.

When I acquired my first live argus the Dyaks never tired of watching and feeding it and showing it off to visiting savages. Again and again they begged me not to go near it at night with my electric flash, for they believed it would die if it ever saw a light at night. When I disobeyed them and it lived I was accredited with still greater powers over creatures of the jungle.

The most delightful of all pets was a tiny sun-bear cub not more than six inches high, black as jet with a perfect orange circle on its chest. We named it Kapit, and even when canned milk became scarce in camp, I would hear the demand from my Dyaks to Mutt, *Kapit mow soosoo,* and it always got a saucerful.

When I returned to Singapore Kapit had gained one whole inch in stature. One day Admiral, then Commander, Eberle called to see my collections. He was in full uniform, and this was in the good old days before governmental terror at possible aristocratic display had ripped off all the gold lace and beauty from these uniforms and clad the officers in the blue serge of the common peepul, thus making democracy and drabness safe. In spite of the glittering uniform, the infant mite of a bear flew at the tall naval officer and fiercely mouthed the end of his scabbard. Taken up in the hand its fury changed at once to resentment at having its ferocious attack spoiled, and thereafter it ceased not to suck its paws and sing dismally to itself. If ever there was a flesh and blood Winnie the Pooh, it was Kapit. It steamed safely back to New York and lived long and happily in the Zoological Park.

Some of the dead argus pheasants brought in were in perfect condition except for having their throats cut, and later I learned how these birds were taken. During the season of courtship the male clears and keeps free of all leaves and jungle debris, a circular dancing arena in the heart of the woods, where he displays his gorgeous feathers to his prospective mates. Into the center of this arena the savages drive a piece of split bamboo, with its characteristic razor-like edges. Along comes the argus, hurrying up the path which leads to his ball-room, with his heart full of the joy of mere physical existence and of the bliss of dancing before his lady. He pauses suddenly at seeing his sanctum defiled by the piece of bamboo, and postpones his loud summons to any hens within hearing until he has cleared the ground. Sooner or later in his struggles with the offending bamboo the poor bird executes himself, committing gular hari-kari with the sharp edges of the upright splinter.

I have spoken of ants, and I had to think of them many times before I left these jungles. In one spot I had the Dyaks dig me a carefully concealed pit in the ground close to a used dancing arena, and here I waited patiently for the coming of the owner. I heard the bird call near at hand and finally a rustle in the underbrush drew my attention, and I was prepared to see the splendid bird step forth and claim his jungle playground, when the fire-ants found me out. These villains work almost wholly at night, and when they discovered my dark hiding place, it must have seemed some wonderful dispensation of the god of ants.

Here was a ready-made hollow, filled with a store of living food. Three or four ant scouts located this manna simultaneously and proceeded to take possession at once in approved fire-ant fashion. The great sharp jaws take the firmest kind of a bull-dog grip, and close fast, giving a splendid purchase for striking full force with the poisonous sting at the opposite end of the body. I am a trained ornithologist; to learn a new fact, to ferret out some hidden habit, I would undergo much pain and cramping of body and limb. But I am also a human being, and the coming of the said pain must permit an appreciable amount of anticipation; must allow at least an instant's bracing of the will, a moment of conscious determination to resist stoically. When one is crouched underground, tense with excitement, with one's whole being concentrated on the external world, and lighted matches are applied simultaneously to several portions of one's anatomy, I doubt if the enthusiast lives who could avoid rising from such a grave without dignity or delay. I think I broke the world's standing high jump record, and as far as I know the argus pheasant is running yet.

A final note about ants. I had promised a friend to bring him whatever jungle mice I could secure, so every evening at camp I would set out a dozen traps or more. While eating dinner, or later when writing my notes, I would hear the snap of a trap, and rushing to it I would find it sprung but empty. I solved the mystery by a patient watch one night,

Kapit, My Sun Bear Cub

He lived for many months in the New York Zoo

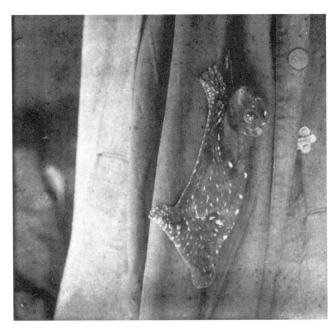

Flying Lemur

A member of the group of Insectivorous Mammals, able to scale through the air for many yards

on its parachute of skin

when I saw two of the huge black fire-ants pull and haul on the bait until they actually sprang the trap, disappearing at once into the surrounding leaves. These ants never bothered us in camp but late at night when I made my way down to the canoe viaduct one or two of them would often nip me and make me dance with pain.

At every Dyak house to which I paid a visit I was received with the greatest courtesy. There was but one tribal house which did not make some advance and offer some friendly salutation. This particular communal dwelling of hostile Dyaks was built at the foot of a steep hill, so that low trees overhung the roof, and gave the structure a fictitiously peaceful air. We had been warned against them, and so passed them by within a discreet radius. My own Dyaks were not wholly at ease as we paddled by on the opposite side of the river. I had them stop for a while and drift, while I rested my most powerful glasses on the gunwale and raked the whole building. In a score of places I could see armed Dyaks peering through the chinks at us, and near one end were the rifle-like muzzles of three blow-pipes pointing our way, with whose poisoned arrows I was already acquainted.

This inhospitality was more than made up at other villages, where often an orderly programme of events was presented in my honor, and the chief and his wives would wear their most precious decorations. I remember with great vividness the day when we landed at the home of Narok, one of the younger men of my crew who had earned considerable distinction among his people as a dancer. On this particular day two men had gone ahead in a fast canoe to give word that a war-canoe manned by thirteen paddlers, and carrying various gifts as well as a white man, would appear in the early evening at an appointed time. At dusk, therefore, when our boat grated against the pebbly beach bordering the jungle where Narok lived, a crowd of men, women, and children, and a still greater host of mongrel dogs, rushed down to greet us. These men and women were like very polite boys and girls at some great celebration. I do not believe that they had ever seen but one white person, and certainly every article included in my equipment, even down to the pots and pans, as well as the last minute detail of my clothing, filled them with unparalleled curiosity. I even think that secretly they were a little amused at such manifestations of an alien culture. But they made no sign to show it. Instead, those of the proper caste came forward silently and gravely to greet us.

This Dyak greeting holds true to the old, primitive ideal that a guest must be welcomed with a gift. This gift is a very modest one, but it is also very valuable. It is an egg. Throughout the whole country, if you find favor in the eyes of a tribe, you are formally presented with an egg on the day of your arrival in their village. And in the heart of Borneo, where food is in the nature of things a more or less undetermined quantity, the possession of an egg is a matter of profound gratitude. Particularly a fresh or proper egg, as Mutt would call it, because at times the Dyaks show a marked preference for high game and preserved eggs—an instinctive, almost racial, preference not easily acquired by a more sophisticated taste. There is always the chance, however, that the gift egg will be a good egg. So the presents of Narok's tribesmen found great favor with us when they were ceremoniously pressed into our left hands, and in exchange we offered our small supply of scissors, mirrors, beads, and flat chocolate wafers wrapped in tin-foil. These wafers did not fail to bring forth sounds of delight, but at the same time they did not fail to provoke a great indecision in the minds of those who had fallen sudden heir to them, because nobody could bring himself to destroy the beautiful, smooth, shining contour of his silver disk, in spite of the chocolate within. It was remarkable to see how momentous this question was to them; to see the real emotion brought out by these scraps of cheap, bright foil that had been of so little value to the civilized people who had produced them.

Narok's home was like all other Dyak communal houses, a wide covered verandah with an open porch in front and a series of single rooms extending all along the back, the whole raised on poles ten to twenty feet above the ground,—this to guard against sudden attacks. Each room sheltered a family and the chief of any village, as we must call these horizontal apartment houses, was known as the Chief of Twenty, or of Sixty Doors, as the case might be.

When the ceremony of landing was fully and properly completed, Narok led me to his tribal house, where, one by one, we all climbed the steep, notched pole that formed the sole roadway between the earth and the lofty verandah, about twelve feet up. I felt most convincingly like a chicken going to roost. This bamboo-floored porch gave directly upon a low-roofed corridor which ran the full length of the dwelling. At intervals resinous fires burned in shallow bowls before a long row of barred doors. Behind these doors the individual members of the tribe lived out the daily routine of their lives in some semblance of seclusion. I would have liked to see the personal possessions gathered in these rooms, but I was conducted to a seat of honor in the direct center of the long corridor, where I sat down on some spotlessly clean mats and awaited the program which was to welcome our coming. Directly above me, suspended from the roof by slender strips of bamboo fibre, hung a circle of dried human heads, each one equally distant from its neighbor. White, wooden eyes had been placed in the eye-sockets of these heads—white eyes unnaturally large and distended. The expression was a bewildered, quizzical one,—they were all staring at something which was hidden in the dark shadows of the inner roof—something inside those mysterious, barred rooms.

Immediately a huge circle formed about us.

WITH THE DYAKS OF BORNEO

From first one door and then another and from the shadows of the gallery beautiful bronze figures like shining, polished statues, great and small, moved with the noiseless tread of the savage, and came and squatted about me, until the circle grew, ring upon ring, like the section of some giant tree. Every eye was fixed upon me in curious, fascinated gaze, and every tongue was busily discussing me in the deep, guttural language of which I understood a word here and there.

The young girls of the tribe put before me all the paraphernalia of betel-nut chewing and a bowl of native tobacco, which they proceeded to roll into plantain-leaf cigarettes. I chose the lesser of the two evils and found the tobacco not at all strong or rank. The circle of which I was the hub had become so vast that I could not have left, if I had desired to do so. And now I closed my eyes for a moment, playing my usual game of what I might call intensifying an experience, and said over and over to myself that this was not any make-believe, nor abnormal, temporary Dahomey or Dyak village in some World's Fair, but the real thing, the only real Borneo, the actual, wild, savage Sea-Dyaks. And also as usual, when I closed my eyes, my other senses became dominant, and the smells reinforced my assertions,—the heavy, not unpleasant, and not negroid odor of the Dyaks themselves, and sifting through all the aromatic fragrance of the burning resin. An overwhelming realization of alien, primitive man, of the elemental vitality of exotic savagery possessed me. For a while the veil was lifted between the present and the far-distant past, and I sensed keenly the life of my savage ancestors, with all its superstitions, its cruelty, and its fitful emotionality.

Without my knowing when it began I became aware of two low throbbing tom-toms, the beat faint and often drowned by other sounds, made by the tapping of fingers on the stretched skins. Then three men struck up the mournful, monotonous music of the native reed flutes, and two little boys strutted in, dressed in all the war regalia of grown-up Dyaks. Never was anything more stately and serious than the bearing of these children. The instinct for war is born in them and from boyhood they are taught to revere and practise it as they do nothing else. Taking from the children the war-coat of bear-skin and hornbill feathers and the cap of red and gold beadwork, with its long, ocellated plumes of the argus pheasant, Narok began to dance. Heretofore I had known him only as one bare back among the other paddlers; now I realized that in his profession he was a great man in his race.

The tom-toms now rose to a deeper and stronger tone, the flute music increased and was as intricate and exact as it was alien to my ears. A rooster among the rafters overhead stirred and crowed sleepily, and this drew my eyes upward. There was no wind, no slightest breeze, but there, close above me, the heads were swaying at the ends of their tethers, and to my startled eyes they seemed to be moving in some terrible rhythm, in time with the war dance which had started.

The tattooed, coppery body of the dancer took a hundred difficult and graceful poses, the spots of light on the hornbill feathers of his coat dancing before my eyes until all my being was concentrated on his swaying, sinuous figure. The great circle ceased to exist for me; nothing seemed to have any reality save the dancer, the sobbing music, and the heavy, alien odor,—and always these eternally waving white spots. The spirit of the savage was now embodied in music and the dance. Above my head—I did not need to look up to see them, I could *feel* their presence—swung the dry and blackened human heads, one of which, I imagined at my last glance, had shifted and now stared vacantly down upon us through white, wooden eyes.

The dancer now sank almost to the ground, his body leaning so far back that the long argus feathers swept the floor. Never ceasing for a moment the swaying, swinging rhythm, with almost an imperceptible movement he picked up his great wooden shield and drew his gleaming sword from the carved sheath at his side. Circling on one foot, the other drawn up above the knee, he spun round and round—faster and faster—until, with a resounding blow of sword on shield, and then a straight outward thrust, he sank to the floor.

This was the beginning of a terrific battle with

an invisible adversary, and the dancer had just parried a fatal blow. Gradually rising, he circled like a great bird with outstretched wings, and the bird was a bird of prey, whirling about a victim for whom there was no escape. The dancing figure whirled and swayed eternally, drawing near and retreating, sinking low to the earth, only to rise again with renewed clashes of sword and shield. I felt a strange drowsiness creeping over me. I knew exactly how Kim felt when he gazed at the water-filled shards of Lurgan Sahib. What was it about which the dancer hovered, whose shape was so illusive that I knew not whether it lay desperately wounded with knife and shield fallen useless beside it, or whether it stood bound to a post? But always its eyes—wooden and white—were fixed upon the swaying figure, and always the white feather spots danced before me, and deep within my brain the blood pounded in tune with the tom-toms. I had a weird sense of feeling all that the shadow figure might have felt. Always it seemed motionless, stunned, fascinated, with a vague gratitude for the hypnotic dance that made the dread end so much easier; the dance which dulled every sense, even the hope that the sword was sharp and the wielder skilful. And then suddenly its face seemed to grow black and shrunken—even as that of the swaying head above me. The dancer sank exhausted to the floor. The music ceased. I glanced sideways at the mass of faces which I had forgotten, and all were staring open-mouthed at the heaving back of the fallen dancer,—the spell had been as strong on them as upon me.

A wretched Dyak cur yelped as he was kicked out of the circle and we were all crying *Bagus! Bagus! najak!*

Only the grim heads above me remained a reality of my strange fantasy, to make me wonder how large a part hypnotism may play in what to us seems a horrible, savage practice—the head-hunting of this people. I was told later that a Dyak is sometimes quite mad for days after taking a head. I realized the infinite tact and strength with which the two English Rajahs of Sarawak—Sir James and Sir Charles Brooke—have striven to abolish this practice, the greatest passion of the Dyaks, having its roots in courtship, and in their ideas of immortality and filial affection.

It was late, for the moon had dropped down below the topmost branches of the jungle, when I went back to the canoe, which was no more than a long, black shadow on the little beach. The men took up their paddles and pushed off, because we had a good distance to cover before morning, and the Dyaks wished to be well down river from the village of hostile savages which we had passed earlier. I stood up amidships and watched the lights of Narok's house become smaller and smaller until they were no more than pin-points of flame in the darkness. I remembered the tribesmen and women who had come to the beach to welcome me, and who had given of their best of hospitality and entertainment to please me. I thought of their simplicity, their utter unsophistication toward life, and compared them with peoples who had learned more complex ways of living. For some reason the simplicity seemed enviable.

I thought too, of all the many people who had furthered the progress of the work which had brought me to their countries; I thought of Ceylon and the white, curved beach of Hambantotta; of the Cinghalese fishermen and their great, unwavering faith in the kindness of the sea; I remembered the Veddahs who had worked so zealously for the success of a trip whose purpose was so obscure and meaningless to them, and I thought that the money paid to them was a very small recompense for their services; there came to mind the jolly Tibetans and the pathetic Hillmen of the western hills; the diverse peoples of the hinterland of Burma and Yunnan, some of them hostile, but others who will live in our kindliest memories forever. And then I looked around with deep sadness at the dim figures of these savage friends, for we were on our homeward journey and in a few days we would separate.

My mood brought home to me the tragedy of this part of all of my expeditions; the meeting with people, alien and strange; the passing through stages perhaps of suspicion, of readjustment, of appreciation, often to real affection; their lives and mine bound closely together for a brief space by ties of interest, respect and danger; to part soon afterward, and live out the remainder of our lives with the round earth between. In civilization friends may go and come again, but when the jungle reaches out and reclaims its people, the whole delicate fabric is unraveled and cannot be woven again. One can never return and find these relations unchanged; life moves swiftly and inevitably, with no sentimental repetition of its successes or failures. As if in proof of this, I looked back and saw the lights in Narok's house go out suddenly— all of them at once, as if a gust of wind had blown them out, while the sudden blackness there seemed to spread slowly toward us, over the trees, and then close down, darker even than night, over the purple stretch of river behind me.

INDEX

A

Afghans, 144, 150
agent, government, 23-25, 193-197
Aladdin, 98-100, 104, 105, 108, 110-113, 129, 139-142, 144, 145, 160, 170, 177, 198, 200-202, 206
Anadenus beebei, 83
Anggun Ana, 167-170
ants, 56, 175, 228, 231, 233
arrows, 127, 128

B

babbler, 93, 185
Balleh, 213
Baloo, 56
bananas, 134-135
banderlog, 67, 90
bats, 173-175, 189
bear, 53, 56
bear, sun, 230
bee-eater, 35, 104, 185
bees, five and six o'clock, 183, 211
beetle, 73
bicycle, 224
boars, 103, 211
boat, Dyak, 212
boat, fishing, 26, 27
boat, native, 14, 15
boulder, 50
bows, cross, 127, 128
"Boy," 29, 32, 40
broadbills, 185
buffalo, 38, 39, 103
bug, kissing, 166
bulbuls, 116, 204
bullocks, 31, 102, 143
bungalow, dak, 98-99
Burong-orang, 217
butterfly, 92, 106

C

Calcutta, 41, 43
canoe, 212-215, 234, 241
carts, bullock, 30
cat-bear, 62
caterpillar, 88
cats, 134
caves, 170-172
centipedes, 175
Ceylon, 13-40, 42
Changthap, 61
Chinaboy, 167-170
Chinese, 124, 129-131, 138, 143, 149, 192
cholera, 193, 202
chowkidar, 31, 32
cicadas, 183, 211
Cinghalese, 21, 22, 28, 142-144, 217, 242
civet-cat, 147
cobra, 135, 136, 193
cock-fight, 149
cockroaches, 172, 174
comet, Halley's, 65, 67, 68, 73, 163
convicts, 192
Cookie, 112, 145, 146, 149, 151, 152, 201, 202, 215, 218, 222
coolies, 152-154
crickets, 121, 163, 193, 203
crocodiles, 199
crows, 22, 79

D

dâk, 98, 99
dance, 148, 238-240
Darjeeling, 43, 45, 46, 48, 152
Das, 46
death, 129, 130, 132
deer, 134, 135
deer, axis, 34
deer, barking, 135, 136

245

INDEX

INDEX

INDEX